Loving Moments

To Mom and Dad,

Thanks for all the loving

moments we've shared.

Ellen

Loving Moments

59 Inspirational Stories
of the Many Faces of Love

COMPILED AND EDITED BY YVONNE LEHMAN

GRACE
PUBLISHING

BROKEN ARROW, OK

LOVING MOMENTS
59 Inspirational Stories of the Many Faces of Love

ISBN 13: 978-1-60495-029-8

From Samaritan's Purse

We so appreciate your donating royalties from the sale of the books *Divine Moments, Christmas Moment, Spoken Moments, Precious Precocious Moments, More Christmas Moments, Stupid Moments, Additional Christmas Moments,* and now, *Loving Moments* to Samaritan's Purse. What a blessing that you would think of us! Thank you for your willingness to bless others and bring glory to God through your literary talents. Grace and peace to you.

Their Mission Statement:

Samaritan's Purse is a nondenominational evangelical Christian organization providing spiritual and physical aid to hurting people around the world.

Since 1970, Samaritan's Purse has helped victims of war, poverty, natural disasters, disease, and famine with the purpose of sharing God' s love through his son, Jesus Christ.

Go and do likewise.
Luke 10:37

You can learn more by visiting their website at www.samaritanspurse.org

Dedication

Dedicated to
Terri Kalfas, who saw the beauty
and value of sharing praise in
Divine Moments
Christmas Moments
Spoken Moments
Precious, Precocious Moments
More Christmas Moments
Stupid Moments
Additional Christmas Moments
and now makes it possible
for the sharing of
Loving Moments

and

to the 50 authors who shared their stories
for this compilation
without compensation
just for the thrill of being useful
and being part of the mission work of
Samaritan's Purse
who receives all the royalties
from the sale of these books

Contents

Introduction
What Is Love?

spoke to a group at church and began with my questions and their immediate answers.

Q: What is the first Bible verse you ever learned?

A: God is love.

Q. What is the first song you learned at church as a child?

A. Jesus Loves Me

Q. Why does God want us to be saved and live with him eternally?

A. Because he loves us.

Next, I asked, "What is love?"

No ready answer came. A few mouths opened, then closed. Questioning eyes fastened on me as if to say, "You're the speaker. Tell us."

The lack of response wasn't because they didn't know, but because there are so many answers at different times and in various situations. Using the same word for the feeling I have for chocolate and for God seems deficient. And yet, I love chocolate and I love God.

"What is love?" is a question mankind has attempted to answer from time immemorial.

When I gave the call-out for *Loving Moments* articles, I knew the end result would provide me with a greater understanding of love. I knew the articles would be varied, meaningful, delightful, and inspiring just as they have been on the themes in the seven other *Moments* books.

Some authors reveal how faith and understanding of love may be strengthened by the almost-overlooked simple things in life. Others experience and appreciate love through times of great suffering and trials.

Love — a valid word that can be applied to…bugs…or our savior dying on the cross for our sins.

I hope you enjoy these *Loving Moments*.

Yvonne Lehman

1
Bonds of Love

Above all these things put on love, which is the bond of perfection.

Colossians 3:14 NKJV

All bonds are breakable — with the exception of one.

Love is the natural bond between humanity and God. Christ's perfection is the unbreakable tie that connects us to God forever. The weight of having to be perfect has been removed from our shoulders through Jesus' sacrifice on the cross. We are now approved in Christ.

As a pastor, I see people deal with various burdens. One is fear, and that fear is a fruit of torment — a torment derived from seeking approval from people or God. People fear rejection, so they don't reach out to achieve their dreams and aspirations. God wants us to achieve greatness, and He has provided an unbreakable bond to Himself to help us achieve it.

Christ is the unbreakable bond. He died for our sins, and when we believe in Him, it creates an indestructible link between us and God. His love is the mortar to the structure as well as the foundation of a great building. We are bound to His perfection and will never again be tossed around by our weaknesses. The bond we have through Christ is eternal and unblemished.

Putting on love requires receiving the love of God through Christ. We are loved by the Lord, and His mercies eclipse our problems. His love is an endless sea of forgiveness that has yet to be explored. The depths of His love have not been fully tested. When we find His love, we find His mercies. By believing in His power, we are transformed into new people and bound to His perfection. His identity becomes ours.

If you are struggling to find worth or merit, the answer involves understanding the bond you have with perfection. Your actions won't always measure up, but through God's love you are connected to His perfection. Put on love and envision the connection you have to perfection through God's love.

Josh Clevenger

2

Lightning Bugs

My three-year-old son, Mason, went to bed screaming, "No! If I go to bed, I will miss the lightning bugs!"

It was one of those amazing spring nights, still warm enough after dinner to go outside in a t-shirt, shorts, and flip-flops. My son insisted on wearing tall socks and his "fast shoes." He pulled the socks up so high he might as well have been wearing pants. The lightning bugs hadn't arrived yet, but he remembered last year very well.

I'm glad he's excited about lightning bugs.

I suspect that it won't be long before he's excited about an all-day fishing trip with his dad, and I will not see him unless I lie on the boat (and I happen to have a huge fear of fishing hooks, no matter how much I trust the person casting).

It won't be long before he can't sleep because he's excited about his first day of school.

It won't be long before he's excited about chasing things that are bigger than lightning bugs, probably things with wings that migrate in the winter or things with antlers that walk in the land behind our house. I will remind him that his mom gets a *little* excited about it too. Maybe he won't listen when his dad tells him that mom only shoots if she can do it off the back porch in her sweatpants and house shoes and that she probably will not join them on their long excursions.

It won't be long before he's excited about staying the night with a friend, eating chips and cookies until he gets sick and making stupid jokes that only ten-year-old boys find humorous.

It won't be long before he can't sleep because he's thinking about that cute girl who just moved to his school. He won't realize that she will not be impressed by him licking the floor for money, or eating a half-eaten peppermint for money, or any other crazy things that his dad thought would be cool when he was his age.

It won't be long before he's serious about that girl and wants to take her to the dance. And he won't realize that his momma doesn't think she is good enough for him. And never will be.

It won't be long before he's getting home late from practice and falling asleep on the couch before throwing his nasty clothes in the laundry room.

It won't be long before he doesn't notice that the lightning bugs are out.

It won't be long before he packs his bags and leaves in search of bigger and better things.

It won't be long before he realizes that all the big things the world has to offer are more frustrating and mundane than he thought they would be. He might find himself wondering what his real purpose is. Hopefully he will discover how much God loves him and wants to give him an abundant life.

It won't be long before he finds his better half who reminds him that the best joys are found in relationships with people who make us want to be better and enjoy the little things. She will remind him of his momma, except that she will be a little more creative and patient with details.

It won't be long before he's tucking in his own little lightning-bug-chaser. And the child will remind him how much he had loved waiting on those delightful little creatures that only an amazing and imaginative Creator could create.

He will remember to enjoy today and not get so caught up in waiting for tomorrow. And that the little childhood joys and childlike faith are qualities that never have to end. In fact, they are what keep us going while we wait for tomorrow.

Kristin Tobin Dossett

3
My Accidental Friend

I distinctly remember my sister-in-law telling me that when my children went to school, their friends' parents would become some of my best friends. I didn't give it much thought until my children started school at a small, private Christian school and I began to be invited to coffee and lunch with other moms on a fairly regular basis. I was getting to know some of them pretty well but hadn't given any thought to them actually being more than good acquaintances.

What I hadn't bargained for was meeting Teresa. As new moms at the school, our paths crossed frequently. We ended up driving in the same car on a couple of field trips and had a chance to talk extensively. I realized that she was smart, fun, funny, and that we had a lot in common.

Every once in a while, we'd be the only ones who showed up for our weekly coffee or lunch and our conversations would last for hours. Sometimes I hoped that nobody else *would* show up so we could continue our great talks. We began sharing our lives with each other on a deeper level. Before long, Teresa had become an integral part of my life. She had crept in and become my new BFF without my even realizing it.

For the past sixteen years, our families have spent many New Year's Eves, July Fourths, Memorial Days, Labor Days and numerous family birthdays together. Her family has helped my family move on numerous occasions (that is true friendship). She has always been there for me with a meal, a card, or just a call or text to check on me.

When my family was struggling financially, she bought my lunch more times than I can remember. Over the years, we've seen our children go from kindergarten to graduating high school and college, and every stage in between. Parenting college students and young adults has been our latest topic of conversation. We've arrived at and survived that scary place we could barely imagine five or six years ago called the empty nest. We are helping each other rediscover our husbands and to become better wives now that our kids are gone. I am sure we will laugh, cry, and pray our way through the territory ahead like we have with every other stage of our lives.

I can't count the times we've laughed so hard we nearly wet our pants or the fact that we've cried together in more public places than I care to think about. She has been my constant prayer partner. Teresa came into my life in an ordinary way when I wasn't really looking for a friend but we have lived life together, the nitty-gritty parts of life that can make or break you. We've raised our children together and made our marriages work together. We've kept each other accountable on so many levels.

The Bible says in Proverbs 18:24 that a man who has friends must himself be friendly, but there is a friend who sticks closer than a brother. This couldn't be truer than with my friend, Teresa. She is the sister I never had, and I couldn't love her more if we were actually blood relatives. I thank God for her every day.

Karen Sawyer

4
Why Do You Love Me?

I saw him on the other side of the roller rink at the church skating party and wondered how to approach him. He had been the guest speaker at my church on Sunday, and I was smitten. Eventually I got up the nerve to skate a little closer to him and say "Hi, I'm Carol."

He smiled, nodded and sped off.

I saw him at various church functions and created the opportunity to double date with him and another girl. I enjoyed his company but assumed he was never going to be interested in me. I had tried. I had failed.

Months went by. Pulling into my driveway on a warm Tuesday afternoon in late summer, I noticed his car parked about a block away. "That's odd, why is Paul in this neighborhood?" I wondered.

No one locked their doors in the 1970s. I went to the back of the house to bring my groceries into the kitchen and there sat Paul. On my sofa. In my living room. Looking sheepish.

Hundreds of thoughts raced through my head...and they were mostly negative. I imagined I had offended him in some way and he was there to tell me off.

What came out of his mouth had me staring at him with my jaw unhinged, unable to speak, and likely looking like an idiot. He said, "I've been watching you for a long time and have grown to like you very much. I was wondering, could we go to dinner sometime?"

I answered, "Uh huh," nodding in disbelief.

We spent the evening chatting and getting to know each other. There was no doubt in my mind. This was the guy I wanted to marry.

He called the next day to tell me he couldn't wait for dinner and was wondering if I would have lunch with him instead.

We met at noon. When the waiter asked us for our order we told him we needed more time. After coming back three times to take our order we told him we weren't hungry. The reason? Paul had just asked me to *marry him* and we still had not had our first date. Could he have been playing hard-to-get all along?

On November 24, 1972 we married in Las Vegas.

Our lives together have been battered, bruised and broken numerous times. The trauma we had to endure is more than any one couple should have to go through.

Last year I received from my husband, normally a man of few words, the following letter:

> I watch you and wonder what I ever did to deserve you. I wonder why you have never left me. I wonder...
>
> When we found out we could never have children, we were able to adopt our son. One year later the mother who tossed him aside wanted him back. We had no choice but to return the child. He was not ours to keep. You were there to convince me we would survive the loss.
>
> For fourteen years I watched you after you received a cancer diagnosis and the doctors confirmed that you would never have children. Although we were able to adopt another boy, you remained strong in your belief that you would one day bear a child.
>
> The miracle happened, just as you said it would. Your pregnancy was risky and there was no assurance you or baby would live. I held your hand when our little girl arrived six weeks early, and surprising everyone, she was perfect.
>
> When our beautiful home was a total loss, destroyed by vandals, you picked up the pieces and assured me we could start over.
>
> When our business partners stole our business including everything we owned, you said, "We've been through worse. We'll make it through this too."
>
> When I was falsely arrested and imprisoned you stood firm, never doubting my innocence. You waited — you stayed.
>
> When I was at death's door for six weeks in China with no communication outside the village, you never gave up hope.

When the police told you they could not find me, you told the children, "Daddy will be home soon, I promise."

When I was in the car accident that left me with brain damage and disabled, you spoon-fed and nurtured me as my sole caregiver for the six years when I couldn't help myself.

When our son and family walked away from us all, I watched a piece of you die. I thought it would destroy you. But after all your tears and anger, you began a campaign of "He will come back. I will never give up hope." You helped me work through the pain of that loss.

You do not pity or patronize me. You do not treat me like an invalid. You just love me. You know my limitations and never ask more of me than I am able to give. You never complain.

You never lost your hope. How could I not love you?

I watch you and I wonder — why do you love me?

I love him more today than I did forty-five years ago. He loved me during the years when we weathered those storms. But any of you who have been married for a long time know that it turns into a different type of love. It is deeper and you only feel complete when you are together.

Carol Graham

5

Count Your Blessings

When I was a little girl, my grandmother would often sing to me. One of her favorites was the old hymn, "Count Your Blessings," which she would croon in a sweet, quavering voice, reciting the lyrics to me:

When upon life's billows you are tempest-tossed,
When you are discouraged, thinking all is lost,
Count your many blessings, name them one by one,
And it will surprise you what the Lord has done.
Count your blessings, name them one by one,
Count your blessings, see what God has done!
Count your blessings, name them one by one,
Count your many blessings, see what God has done.

Although I did not realize it at the time, by singing those lyrics to me, my grandmother was teaching me to focus on the good things that were in my life, regardless of the circumstances. She had borne many hardships in her life — the untimely death of people close to her, numerous bouts with cancer, the loss of her husband's business, multiple house fires resulting in extensive damage and the loss of property — yet, through it all, maintained a constant choice to look for the best in every person and every situation.

Grandma's sweet spirit was not one which could be mistaken for weakness, but an innate indomitable strength that was not tainted by a negative outlook on life. Regardless of the hardship that she faced, Grandma continued to count her blessings, readily encouraging her grandchildren to do the same.

Although I cannot claim the same sweetness as my precious Grandma, I took her counsel to heart, and have tried to keep my blessings in the forefront of my mind, regardless of the circumstances.

When my unborn daughter was diagnosed with a potentially life-threatening birth defect, I counted my blessings, which meant that regardless of the outcome, I had been given the precious gift of her life for however long she would be with me.

When she was born prematurely, required emergency surgery, and an an extensive hospital stay, I counted my blessings that she had been born alive, was breathing, and fighting for her existence.

When I experienced heartbreaking miscarriage after miscarriage, I counted my blessings that I had the love and support of my husband and daughter.

When my husband was called to fight overseas during wartime, I counted my blessings that I had a husband who wanted to fight for his country, and a supportive community at home.

When my son was diagnosed with autism, I counted my blessings that I had been given the priceless gift of a truly unique child.

When we experienced a period of intense financial hardship, my husband and I counted our blessings that we had always been provided for before, and knew that God would come through for us again.

Sometimes it was hard to remember to count my blessings in the midst of overwhelming grief and hardship. At those times, my family encouraged me to do so, reminding me of the good things in my life that I had either overlooked or had forgotten. That helped more than I can say to redirect my thoughts, reminding me of what truly mattered in my life, and helping me focus on what was good rather than what was not.

Since hardships often erupt into our lives with unwelcome violence and then slowly fade from their painful prominence, it is important to keep a balanced perspective. By choosing to remember the good things in life, such as family, friends, provision, simple joys, and moments of delight, the grief and worries will not be as overwhelming.

By remembering to count our blessings, especially in the midst of life's storms, we will be able to remember the joys, provisions, and gifts with which we have been graced, and help others maintain an attitude of gratitude.

Although it may seem like an overly simple thing to do, my Grandma had it right in singing that hymn over and over to her grandchildren, and in living those lyrics. Those loving moments are some of my greatest blessings that I will forever treasure.

Marybeth Mitcham

6

Furry Alarm Clock

"Woof!"

I groaned and rolled over, hiding my face from Patti, my twenty-pound Lhasa Apso. I pulled a pillow over my head, wishing for just a few more moments of sleep.

"Woof!"

"Aw, Patti, go back to sleep!"

Nelson glanced at the alarm clock, realized it was only ten minutes until rising time, and threw back the covers, saying, "That dog is going to start sleeping in the garage, I'm telling you." He stomped down the hallway.

"You're right, there's no hitting the snooze button in this house."

I grabbed my robe and slid it over my shoulders. "Come on, Patti, let's get you outside."

I led her to the front door, opened it, and watched the shaggy little dog make her way to her favorite tree. As I waited, the smell of freshly brewed coffee drifted from the kitchen. I rubbed my eyes, wondering what I should say to my husband about our furry alarm clock — the one who insisted on waking us at the same time every morning. Even on weekends.

He used to think the dog was a blessing.

"You know Patti loves you," I said to Nelson's back, as he poured his coffee.

He turned and handed me a cup. "Yeah, that helps."

"And we can't make her sleep somewhere else, it would break her heart. Remember that morning the electricity was off and she kept us from being late to work?"

Nelson rolled his eyes. "Yeah, I love the little mutt, but I wouldn't mind sleeping in a few times while we're away." He grinned. "Patti can bark up a storm every morning at the kennel."

I sipped my coffee, the flavor rich to the taste, and sighed.

The following week Nelson and I dropped Patti at the local dog and cat hotel, and drove four hours to a seaside resort. We checked into a deluxe hotel suite with all the trimmings, spent the day sightseeing and fell into the king-sized bed just after midnight.

"Rinnngggg!"

Nelson lifted the phone and said, "Yeah?"

An automated voice greeted him. "Good morning, this is your wake up call..."

He slammed the phone onto the base and turned over. "Did we request a wake up call?"

"No." I yawned. "But look at the time."

It was the exact time Patti always woke us.

"Unbelievable," Nelson said. Later he spoke with the front desk, who apologized for the programming error in the wake up system. We continued our vacation.

"Rinnngggg!"

We received a wake up call, at the same time, every morning for the duration of our stay.

"Rinnnggg!"

"This is eerie," I said, glancing at the clock again. "I can almost feel a paw on my shoulder. Maybe Patti misses us so much that she's still waking us up. By love."

Nelson sighed heavily, answered the phone one last time.

"Good dog."

Robin Bayne

7

A Special Goodbye

Your baby can't live."

Those four words changed my life in ways I would never imagine. But, first I had to accept them.

"He's alive," I told the doctor. "He's kicking right now." I reached across the desk between us. "Here. Feel."

The woman I had come to love like a sister took my hand, but instead of following my tugs, she held on firmly.

"I know he's alive." Were those tears in her eyes? "He has a condition called…"

I know now what she said, but then it seemed like my heart had broken into shards of glass determined to slice through my body.

"Do you understand?"

"He's alive," I repeated as I yanked my hand away from hers. "He's not going to die."

The next few hours seem like a shadowy world I didn't want to inhabit. Somehow, my husband was there. His grip was so tight on my hand, my fingers turned an angry shade of reddish purple.

Finally, different words woke me up. "If you carry him much longer, there's a good chance you'll die. Your sons need their mother."

My sons. My world revolved around those two, only four and seven years old. I couldn't take anything away from them. I listened.

A rare condition called anencephaly had prevented our baby's spinal column from closing, so his skull and part of his brain didn't develop. If born alive, he likely would have basic motor skills, such as swallowing and breathing, and there was nothing to protect him from pain when he came through the birth canal. About three days was the longest a baby born with this condition had lived, and she just lay in an incubator.

Maybe I should have thought of other parents and asked about his chances of being born alive to donate his organs. The doctor put a stop to that before it even fully formed in my mind. "You have too much fluid. It's already showing signs of infection. If we don't get it out of there, I'm afraid we'll lose you."

"We can't lose her." My husband, usually soft-spoken, didn't hesitate.

"I won't have an abortion." That much, I knew. I didn't, and still don't believe in abortion for any reason.

"I won't give you one," my doctor assured me. "What we would do is induce labor. You would go through a natural labor and give birth."

"I'm almost seven months pregnant. Will he live?" I still held onto the hope she was wrong.

"He may live a few moments after he's born."

"We have to do this," my husband said.

Twenty-seven years old, and the mother of two children, I said the first thing that came to my mind. "I want my mom."

After more technical talk we made plans for first thing Wednesday morning, which gave my family a couple days to make arrangements, and drive almost one-hundred miles to get to us.

The next few days, I couldn't get close enough to my sons. The oldest never minded if I cuddled, but the youngest would usually have none of that.

Not then. He sensed something was wrong and gave me hugs and all the contact I could want.

The day before I was scheduled to go in, my doctor called and asked if we could come to her office for a brief time. She just wanted to talk to us.

Leaving our sons home with my parents and sister, who arrived that afternoon, we went to her office.

"Your church is between pastors, isn't it?"

Her words threw me for a loop. "Yes."

I can still see the sunlight reflected off myriad shades of amber hair as she nodded. "Can I talk to you about God?"

Believe it or not, I wasn't angry with God. I wasn't happy with him, either. I just didn't want anything to do with him at the moment. But something about the look on her face made me say, "Yes."

"Your heart is broken right now, but I promise someday you'll hold this baby. He'll be healthy and happy, and you'll be with him throughout eternity."

"Does he have a soul?" I had scoured the Bible, looking for an answer.

"Of course, he does. God created his soul right along with his body."

Then, I finally asked *the* question. "Did I do something wrong to make this happen?"

"No," my husband spoke, just as the doctor said the same word.

She then explained the theories about the condition, none of which had ever been proven. The main thing was they had never found a commonality between mothers, either, so I hadn't done anything to cause this. At least not physically.

I was too scared to ask the next questions. What had I done that God was punishing me for? Was I not a good mother to the children he'd already blessed me with? Was I a bad person? Had I committed some great sin and not asked forgiveness? I was afraid of what her answer might be.

She spoke for a while about God and heaven, and when we left, I felt better about what would happen to our baby. I still wasn't sure about me, though.

The morning came. I went in, shaking so hard my teeth rattled. My mother and husband were with me, and my dad and younger sister stayed back to give my sons as normal a day as possible. The nurse had to help me into my gowns because I could barely stand. Was this what it felt like on death row, knowing no miracle would come along to save us. Dark thoughts filled my head and began to take over.

As I lay waiting for the injection into my IV, my mind raced. I must have done something wrong. Maybe I hadn't thanked God enough for my boys. Maybe I needed to be a better wife, daughter, or person. I didn't deserve another child.

Then my doctor came in. After expressing sympathy to my husband and mother, she walked over to me. "I'm going to pray before I inject this."

I didn't care. Pray away. God didn't care about me. He wouldn't have done this if he did. He only liked perfect people, not those of us who make mistakes all the time.

Then her words sank in. "Comfort her, and let her feel the peace that only you can give her right now. Give her the knowledge that you will hold her baby in your hands when he leaves her. And, Lord, please let her say goodbye to him."

I'd like to say peace settled over me right away, but I'd be lying. Instead, I stopped my internal ranting to focus on her final words. What could she mean about saying goodbye to my baby? Couldn't I just talk to my stomach? Wasn't I still going to see him before she took him away? I could tell him then, couldn't I?

My mom began crying as the doctor injected the medication into my IV. Within thirty minutes, I was in labor. It was twice as painful as either of my other sons. Of course, that may have been because I knew he wouldn't be there to hold and take care of when this was over.

Nonetheless, the pain was incredible. Then, my doctor was there again. I can hear her as clearly as if she were standing beside me right now. "I can't do more for your inner pain, but I can help your physical pain."

"Please," I begged her.

She injected something into my IV again, and within minutes, the pain was better. I felt numb. Physically, I mean. Inside, I was still screaming for this to not be real. For this to be a nightmare I would wake up from at any moment.

I drifted in and out of consciousness, hearing my mom and husband talk.

My mother told somebody she was proud of my strength. I wanted to scream out that I wasn't strong. I was terrified. I didn't want this to happen. But, I couldn't form a coherent word.

Then, after what seemed like days but was actually eight hours, something I will never forget happened. Peace came over me, and the drugs no longer inhibited my thoughts. Then, I felt it —loving hands reached into me and came away, holding my perfect little boy. They stayed over me for a moment.

"Goodbye, baby." A tiny face turned toward me. "I love you, and I'll hold you someday."

As though drawing him to a chest, the hands went higher and disappeared.

"What's going on?" my husband asked.

I looked at a very confused pair of people. "Our son just died. I told him goodbye."

My mother thought something was seriously wrong with me so she went for the doctor. When I told her what had happened, she smiled. "God answered my prayer for you."

The prayer I hadn't understood.

25

She picked up her stethoscope. "I don't need to do this, but for the record..."

Her eyes met mine as she probed my still large stomach. "No heartbeat. He's gone."

I looked at my mom, who was crying. My husband's eyes were moist with tears begging to be released. Why were they upset now? Hadn't I just told them wonderful news? My baby was with God! I tried to soothe them. "It's okay. God has him. He came and let me say goodbye to our baby. It's okay."

Within minutes, his lifeless body came into the world. He looked like a miniature version of his two older brothers, so utterly beautiful. At least, what I saw.

For legal reasons, my husband and mother had to look at everything. My mom understandably broke down. My husband couldn't hide his agony for a moment. But, ever strong for me, he stepped to the side of the bed and took my hand.

"He wouldn't have lived." His fingers tightened on mine. "We did the right thing."

"I know."

And I did.

Yes, I spent months crying off and on, wanting to hold my baby. And, yes, I still find myself wondering if I was somehow the cause.

But one thing I have never doubted — whether or not anyone else believes it — God showed me he held my little boy.

God let me tell my baby goodbye.

Georgia Florey-Evans

Author's Note: Two years ago, we put up a memorial stone on our family cemetery plot. That helped me more than anything else we've done. Our pastor and entire families came and we had a short service celebrating the little boy who was here for such a brief time. Now, I can put flowers out there when I'm thinking about him. His name is John Lucius Evans, named after my grandfather.

Praying this story touches somebody and helps them heal.

8

A Valentine for Jesus, My Bridegroom

Dear Jesus,

You sent me a valentine written in crimson blood. It says, "I have loved you with an everlasting love" (Jeremiah 31:3). You have also said in Your Word that nothing can separate me from Your love (Romans 8:38-39).

This year I want to give You a valentine from my heart. What kind would You like? Would one of these *hearts* delight You?

A faithful, undivided *heart* that puts You first each day. (Matthew 6:33)

A sincere *heart* that bows before You in worship and praise. (Psalm 95:6–7)

A true *heart* that loves You with wholehearted devotion. (1 Chronicles 29:19)

A giving *heart* that is other-centered, not self-centered. (Philippians 2:4)

A loving *heart* that is patient, kind, and forgiving. (1 Corinthians 13:4–5)

A devoted *heart* that sings, "My Jesus, I love Thee, I know Thou art mine." (See Psalm 18:1).

Lord Jesus, this Valentine's Day I want to renew my love for You. Please help me remain faithful to You and always put You first in my life. Thank You for Your incredible love for me. Help me love You more each day.

Your beloved bride,

Lydia

That's the kind of Valentine we can give God — a changed heart when needed. We can renew our commitment to love and cherish him.

We may sing a love song from our heart, say a prayer of gratitude, or write a love letter or poem to show our devotion. Whatever we give from our heart, God will accept with joy. "As a bridegroom rejoices over his bride, so shall your God rejoice over you." (Isaiah 62:5 NIV)

How beautiful to know that we can express our love for God and rejoice in His great love for us.

Lydia E. Harris

9

Never Too Late
to Come Home

"Your mother called."

I raised a questioning eyebrow at my coworker. That didn't seem likely. You see, I had not spoken with my mother in over three years.

Our relationship had become tenuous when she warned me of the man in my life. However, I was too stubborn and rebellious to listen to the guidance she offered. I wish I had heeded her advice. The last years with that man had been nothing but a living torment. He had slowly taken everything from me, including breaking all ties with my family. I was broken and at the end of my rope. On more than one occasion I begged God to show me the way out.

Earlier that day, I'd had a huge argument with the man I lived with. I was tired of the emotional rollercoaster and had reached my limit. Declaring I would not return to this suffocating existence I reached out to the only person that had been there with me through the last three years, my heavenly father. "Father, give me a sign. Show me what I'm supposed to do. Do I continue to live like this? If not, then how do I free myself of this albatross?"

Several hours later, I answered the phone at my place of employment. I was moved to tears and completely astonished to hear the voice of my mother. I couldn't believe how reassuring it felt to hear the voice of someone who cared about me. In that instance, I knew God had sent me the sign I requested. I had faith that He would show me the way out of this mistake.

I was nervous to speak with Mama. I had no idea what to expect. Instead of berating me, putting me down or telling me I should have listened, I was met with words of love and wisdom. She said, "Let's put the past behind us and start over."

I was astonished to be treated with such love. All I'd heard for the past three years were insults and lies. My head had been filled with deception and falsehoods about my family wanting nothing to do with me. Now that I was speaking with my mother, I realized the truth. I was loved by my family.

For my safety, I kept the conversations and relationship with Mama secret for the next two months. Even while the man in my life continued to fill me with lies, God was revealing the truth and opening my eyes.

Two months later, I walked out of that relationship forever. When I called Mama to tell her I was in a safe place, I could hear both the concern and relief in her voice. We both had a lot of unanswered questions.

A week later, my mother appeared in the doorway and we were able to have a face-to-face conversation. She listened while I talked and shared my experience. She never once said, "I told you so," but I'm sure she wanted to.

The next day, I returned home with Mama. We had to adjust to living with one another. I appreciated her kindness and love. She gave me the space I needed, never pushing but allowing me to share when I felt ready.

I was nervous and worried about the reception I would receive from the rest of the family. However, Mama wasn't the only one to welcome me home. My grandmother opened her arms wide and allowed me to walk into them. Her embrace revealed the love she had for me and how much she'd missed me.

The reception from the remainder of the family was also welcoming and loving. Some family members picked up where we left off, as if there had never been an extended absence. With other family members, we had to work through the awkwardness.

Healing did not happen immediately. In some instances it took years. There were times when I exploded and erupted from hurt and anger, but I was still met with kindness and love. Over time I was able to build stronger and deeper relationships than we had before our separation.

I discovered a mother's love is unconditional, especially a mother who lifts her child before the heavenly throne. I discovered later that my mother, grandmother and a hosts of other family and friends fervently prayed for me during that difficult time in my life.

My experience reminds me that I am not worthy of being loved. However, there is One who loves me unconditionally. He was there with me through the bad and has been with me through the healing journey as well.

I may not be worthy of Jesus' love, but he allowed himself to be humiliated and hung on a cross for my sins. All to prove to me just how much he loves me. Because of his sacrifice I am forgiven of my sins. Thankfully, he did not stay on the cross or in the tomb. He arose from the tomb, and is alive and well today, sitting at the right hand of God the father.

He loves me and seeks to have a deeper relationship with me.

Do you know my Jesus? He loves you and wants a relationship with you.

Diana Leagh Matthews

10

Unspoken Love

My two brothers and I always knew Dad loved us deeply. He didn't say so. He didn't need to. His actions and quiet demeanor demonstrated it better than all the words in our tattered Webster's dictionary. Dad worked long hours, sometimes six days a week, providing for us as a logger in the woods near Darrington, Washington. Yet no matter how tired he might be, he always had a smile, a story, and a listening ear for his family.

Unlike parents who play one another against each other, Dad and Mom were a united front. If we asked Mom about going to a movie she invariably said, "See what Dad says." If we approached Dad, his reply was, "What does Mom think?" No chance of wheedling in that setup!

When we were given gifts, they came from both of our parents — until my seventeenth birthday. October 1, 1952 fell on a Wednesday. The Saturday before, Dad announced at the breakfast table, "We are going to Everett today."

I stared. Everett was fifty long miles away. Except for an annual Christmas shopping excursion, we seldom went from our small town to the big city.

"Why are we going?" I asked.

Dad's ocean-blue eyes twinkled. "Wait and see."

I tried to figure out the reason for the trip all the way to Everett. On the Saturdays Dad didn't log, he cut wood for our stoves, fixed whatever needed repaired around the house, and tinkered with a multitude of things that always needed attention. Why were we going to the city when there was so much work waiting at home?

What seemed like an eternity later, we reached Everett. Dad drove the length of the main street and parked at a large stationery store. I blinked. What were we doing here, of all places?

Dad turned and looked at me with such love that I felt tears crowd behind my eyelids. "This birthday gift is just from me, Colleen," he quietly said. "I want you to pick out a Bible. Any one you want."

My heart thumped. We all used our worn family Bible. All I had ever owned was a small red Testament from the Gideons who visited our class at school and gave Testaments to the children.

We stepped into the store. I had never seen so many Bibles! At last I chose a sturdy, red-letter King James Version with a black imitation leather cover. The store inscribed my name in gold letters on the front cover. I reverently clutched my new Bible. Precious in itself, it also represented sacrifice. Dad had given me a day when he could have accomplished a great many pressing chores at home. A day I would never forget.

The Bible is still my most tangible possession. I had it re-covered in black leather when the worn cover fell apart. My name is again inscribed in gold letters. Pages are discolored and bear a wealth of notations, but the old Book is what I would most hope to save in case of disaster.

It is also the only gift I ever received just from Dad, and brings back that autumn day in 1952 when my father gave me a gift of love…and of himself.

Colleen L. Reece

Dear Mammaw

You would think I'm over the top for crying right now.
Seriously. I was only doing the dishes.

Actually I wasn't. And that's the real reason I'm crying. Mason begged to do the dishes. Why does that seem so fun when you're three-years old? I should be more excited than I am about this. I reluctantly agreed that it was time to let him try.

I brought the water to a perfect temperature. I was holding my towel, prepared to clean up more than one splash in the six-foot radius around the sink. I was ready.

Until I poured the soap. It was then that I completely lost it.

In my memories, I was standing in the chair at your kitchen sink, Grandmother, staring at the snow globe keychain and the bunny figurine on your windowsill overlooking the clothesline out back. I felt so privileged to be standing at your sink, with your dishrag, washing your dishes.

You trusted me.

Why was it so fun to do the dishes at your house?

I wish you could see these boys. You wouldn't mind the mess that I'm trying so hard to prevent. We just ate at your table, the one with the crack around the edge of the entire perimeter that I hate because it collects, and keeps, all the crumbs from the past three meals. I still have your aprons in the end-drawer. I can't bring myself to use them, but the boys like to play with them.

Doing dishes.

It's the most ordinary act I will do today, but tonight it sparks the greatest emotion. Everyday tasks are so mundane, so tedious until they transport us back to a place where we wish we could still visit.

I suppose you had more patience than I do now. Maybe that's because you were a grandma and grandmas seem to possess a different level of tolerance when it comes to small children and their inevitable messes.

I felt like the princess in your little brick castle. I felt like life was perfect. It's the same feeling I get when I see morel mushrooms or fried squash, even though I have yet to meet anyone else who knows how to cut or fry them correctly. You really could have had your own cooking show.

It's the same feeling I get when I wash dishes. It's not quite as awesome now that I don't have to stand in the chair, but I think you're smiling down on the one who is. And even though that chair ended up covered in suds tonight, I don't think you would have minded.

Because of you and those memories, I'm reminded every day that life is short, lives are valuable, and the moments are worth even the greatest messes.

Kristin Tobin Dossett

The Greatest Love
I Will Ever Know

My life has been blessed with love. The first eyes I looked into still are filled with love, and light up every time I see her. At 97, my mother, Miss Lu, is a woman of grace, intellect, talent, gratitude, and love.

My husband, Dave, proposed to me on one knee, saying words I cannot remember, but when he said them, they sliced through every fear I had of a future together and sent me into his arms with a resounding, "Yes."

My sister, Judy, came to my aid when I had shoulder replacement surgery. A cancer survivor in her mid-seventies, who hates to travel and loves her own quiet routine, she came for six weeks to help me and my mother. Hers was a true sacrifice of generous love.

Her daughter, my niece, Beth, in the middle of an extremely busy life of work and service, flew in for a few days to lend us her moral support and love.

My pastors, church, and friends have rushed to my side in the rare incidents when I've cried out in need. Following my husband's death, one acquaintance, Holly, called me every morning at 9:00 A.M. to help me start my day. That gift of love grew into an enduring friendship.

I have many other strong friendships with women. The one with Judy has lasted 50 years. We don't always agree on things, but continue to appreciate the value of our relationship.

People have written and spoken to me about how my published books have inspired and touched their lives, helping them find comfort and make wise choices. Many have bought my books, passed them on to family members, friends and co-workers. Some have left reviews on sales sites for the benefit of other readers. That has filled my heart with the love they offer.

I could go on, filling page-after-page, showing the love between parent-and-child, spouses, siblings, friends, pastors, even strangers. But the greatest true love story of my life is the one I'll tell you now.

In October 2008, my husband, who was on medication to retard the progression of the beginning stage of dementia, decided to run out and bring home barbecue sandwiches for lunch.

I was grateful he could still drive short distances, even do a little grocery shopping for me, and usually find his way back home. He still sang in the choir, with help from Leigh, a patiently loving director, and choir members who stood beside him helping him stay on the correct page of the music.

After lunch that day, Dave returned to the family room to his brown leather recliner, one of two matching ones that sat side-by-side. An hour later I heard a crash. I ran into the room and saw Dave situated in an odd, twisted position between two chairs. "What happened?" I asked.

There was no response to my cry. His eyes were open and he was looking at me but it appeared he couldn't move. I called next door and my neighbors came running. After they lifted Dave back into his chair, we asked him to smile, raise his arms, move his eyes, to see if he had experienced a stroke. Shortly after, the neighbors left, with assurances they would return if needed. I told Dave, "I'm going to call an ambulance."

"No, no ambulance," he insisted. "Bring me your mother's old walker."

His face was not drooping, he could talk, see, and smile, which was all good. I brought him the walker, thinking that perhaps he had just lost his balance.

I helped him up, which took a lot of effort, holding on to the back of his pants at the waistband as we maneuvered into the bedroom, where he indicated he wanted to rest.

We got to the end of the bed and his legs gave out. He collapsed onto the floor. I put a pillow under his head and covered him with a blanket to keep him warm. I told him I was calling an ambulance.

Again, he protested but agreed I could call Margaret, our church nurse and friend. Margaret said simply, with no room for exception, "Call an ambulance."

So I did.

Dave had suffered a massive, frontal lobe, cerebral hemorrhage. There was no possibility of recovery. He was given twenty-four hours to live. I called his children. Later that first night, before they arrived, I sat alone in the patient area outside the Intensive Care Unit.

I noticed a large Bible on a corner table. I felt numb, exhausted, sad, and confused by the events, yet a voice inside me niggled, "What good is a Bible when it is closed?"

With great effort, I walked to the table, and randomly opened the Bible. My eyes, and my heart, took in Psalm 42:11: "Why am I discouraged? Why so sad? I will put my hope in God! I will praise him again — my Savior and my God!" (NLT)

I knew God was speaking to me. I wasn't in control, he was. I should not be so sad, or confused; instead I should trust in his love, in his plan, and turn Dave and me over to him.

I did.

Then the children came. John had driven through the night from Washington, DC. Janet, Carol, Debbie, Stephen and his wife Patty, arrived the next day after driving from Pennsylvania and New York.

I was graced through those next days, observing the joy shared between Dave and his friends and family members, in person and on the phone. I was surrounded by and embraced with love, and encouragement. Most days my only prayer was, "Help." At times, I didn't know what I wanted.

God did.

After seven days the children left, needing to return to jobs. That night, as I was sitting beside Dave, with his sister, Marge, and brother-in-law, Shad, Dave's arm stretched forward to something unseen by us. After a few moments I ducked under his outstretched arm, and lay against his chest. He enfolded me in a gentle hug, the last I would receive from the arms that had held me for so many years.

The next day Marge and Shad went home, replaced by Dave's brother Larry, and wife Peg, who had come to care for, and support me. Dave, then in a coma, was transferred to Hospice. Larry and Peg took me out to eat. When I returned to Hospice, Dave's body was shutting down. I could not do this alone. I called friends, Lee and Linda, and they were there in mere minutes, followed shortly by Dr. Leonard, our pastor.

The final hours I spent sitting close to Dave, with my hand on his arm, whispering into his ear, assuring him of the honorable and good man that he was, reinforcing that God and his angels were waiting for him in heaven, and comforting him with declarations that I would be okay. A moment before he left me, his eyes moved toward me, and our final loving contact was made.

With his last breath I experienced the greatest love I will ever know. A veil of peace fell over me, the peace that passes all understanding. The peace that only God can give to those who love him. Thank you, God.

If you are moved by this story, I am grateful, for it is a moving story. If you are saddened by this story, don't be. It is a story of great mercy and great love, a love that sustains me, like King David expressed in Psalm 63:3: "Your unfailing love is better to me than life itself; how I praise you!" (NLT)

Toni Armstrong Sample

13

The Stiff Dog
and the Silly Monkey

Betty Sue, my red-headed twenty-year-old cousin, traveled to my childhood home for an overnight visit. My younger brother and I heard the car pull into the driveway.

"Betty Sue's here!" We ran to the door to meet her. When we saw the two stuffed animals in her arms we knew they were for us.

"Look at you two! How much you've grown!" Our parents came to the door and joined in greeting Betty Sue. My brother and I kept looking at the stuffed animals in her arms. Finally, she took the beautiful stuffed dog, which I knew she was going to give to me, and said to my brother, "Vernon, this one is for you."

Then she took the stuffed monkey and said, "And this one is for you, Janice."

My smile turned into a deflated sigh. The beautifully groomed dog with the soft puffs of fur now belonged to my brother. I was stuck with the silly stuffed monkey.

I wondered about my cousin's thinking. Why would she give my brother, a boy, the prettier of the two stuffed animals? My brother was younger and seemed more like a monkey than I. And I sure did not feel like giving thanks for the silly monkey. I wanted to cry, but tried not to show my feelings.

My brother sat his perfectly poised pooch on top of the chest of drawers in his room. Each time I went by his room my eyes landed on that stuffed dog. The pain continued to be fresh for weeks after Betty Sue left. I would have tried to swap with my brother except I wanted to honor my cousin's decision.

My hurt began to dissolve when I discovered the monkey was huggable. Each day while I was at school, he rested on my bed by the pillow. His brown and beige fur highlighted his sweet face that greeted me on good days and bad days.

Later as a teenager, with all the ups and downs, the monkey comforted me. I did not have to verbalize my hurts to the monkey. I could just hug him. I never gave him a name. I just called him "Monkey."

The beautiful stuffed dog sat stiffly on the furniture in my brother's room. I no longer wanted it because I had discovered my monkey, like the Velveteen Rabbit in the children's book, had worth greater than outward beauty. Monkey had worth known only to my heart.

The dog was eventually tossed out. Monkey ended up going to college with me. He gave me joy and helped me deal with loneliness while far from home. Although Monkey did not get any smarter at college, I no longer thought of him as silly.

Recently Betty Sue died from cancer, and I thought about the wise choice she made in giving me Monkey. I mentioned the stuffed animals to my brother. At first he didn't remember the dog or that Betty Sue had brought the gifts. Truly, his stiff stuffed dog that caused my coveting held no place in his heart.

I am sad that I never told Betty Sue what her gift meant to me during all those years. Now, I can only tell Betty Sue, "Thank you," when I see her in heaven.

Every good gift and every perfect gift is from above and comes down from the Father of lights, with whom there is no variation or shadow of turning.

James 1:17 NKJV

Janice S. Garey

14
Chasing God

I know God is there. I can almost feel his breath on my face when I'm refusing to do what he asks. Or is it just the gentle wind?

I know he's calling. Sometimes his voice is so clear. I know he's talking to me. But sometimes I resist for fear I'll strike out on the wrong path and misread his signals once more. Is that you Lord? Is that your will or just mine again?

Sometimes, I'm not quite sure I hear him, but still, I can't help but chase after God. Sometimes I cry out to him and I know he hears me. My prayers are kept in a bowl up in heaven. Mine is a big bowl. The kind my mother made homemade bread in. My prayers rise like dough. Before I'm finished down here on earth, God may need to have his angels rustle up a second bowl for me. Perhaps even a third. My prayers run over.

In olden days, kings and priests were anointed with God's own recipe of anointing oil. They knew without a doubt why they had been anointed, why they were called. They heard from God through their prophets.

Curious about this anointing oil, I read every God-breathed word about the recipe in the Old Testament.

This recipe was not to be copied and used by any regular Joe-Blow. However, I wanted to know what God's special anointing oil smelled like. I wanted to get a whiff of the Divine's cologne.

The Book of Ephesians says Christians are God's royal priesthood now. Saints. All of us saints. I reasoned I had a right to at least smell the fragrant anointing oil, and if I was at least semi-obedient — for we are all sinners — wear it. So while at my sister's home during the Christmas holidays, I whipped up a batch of anointing oil in her kitchen.

When my nephew's friend, Josh, came over for a visit, he asked me what I was up to. I told him. "But I'm leaving out one ingredient, just in case," I said, winking. "I wouldn't want to incur the wrath of God."

He went upstairs and told my nephew, "David, your aunt is downstairs whipping up a batch of anointing oil."

David replied, "I hope she doesn't blow up the kitchen!"

So little faith has this younger generation.

When I'd finished mixing olive oil with cassia, cinnamon, and myrrh, I and the curious around me decided God's anointing oil smelled just like Christmas — the birth day of Christ. Why were we surprised?

Thrilled, I continued chasing God.

Sometimes, I found others who had heard from Him.

Johnny Cash was one. I'd never particularly cared for the country singer's music, although I'd grown up listening to his songs because my parents liked him. I couldn't figure out why the Holy Spirit was coaxing me to see the movie *Walk the Line*. But, for some strange reason, I was hooked on Johnny Cash after I saw the movie.

When visiting a church at Biltmore in Asheville, North Carolina, I discovered a young preacher who was also enamored. He mentioned Johnny's brother saying something like, "I have to study the Bible, J.R. I can't help nobody if I don't know what it says."

After buying Johnny's autobiography, I knew why I was supposed to delve into his life. His walk on this earth was all about character change. But instead of being about a patriarch from the Old Testament, his story was more contemporary. Relevant. The story was about a changed man...and the takeaway was that no matter how big a sinner I am, as long as I repent and turn back to God, I can be used. Even in this day and time, God keeps calling us.

The most fascinating story in Cash's book was about a little Jewish boy who was taken to the First Baptist church on 57ᵗʰ Street in New York City because he insisted that Johnny Cash was going to be there. He wanted to worship with him.

Johnny and his wife, June Carter, happened to be in New York that same Sunday, walking down that same street, and happened to walk into the First Baptist church by chance. Or was it Divine appointment?

They'd never noticed the church before that visit. When the little boy saw them he jumped up and down announcing, "I told you! I told you he was coming!" The only vacant seats were next to the boy. The Jewish parents said they had brought him to that church because that's where he said Johnny Cash would be coming.

Only God could have arranged that appointment.

The Holy spirit kept giving me a taste of bread crumbs to keep me hungering for more, following where he led, where others had also walked leaving a trail to follow — so I would know the stories of other ambassadors for Christ who had also chased after God with a longing to catch a glimpse of his face.

When I read about Bruce Olsen who had come to know the Lord at age fourteen while hungering for God's will over his life, I was amazed at how he chased God all of the way to South America. He gave up hope to go to college to be a linguist because God told him to teach the murderous Motlione Indians about Jesus. Without a mission board for backing, the nineteen-year-old left with seventy dollars in his pocket to walk into the unknown, not even speaking Spanish.

He fought God at first. Rebellious like most. He made up every excuse to talk himself out of going. But in the end, God won. Olsen wrote, "I had forgotten how hard God can make it on someone who won't do what he's told."

His story made me tremble to think that God would call me to go to the jungle. With only seventy dollars? I wasn't adept at trekking around in high humidity and heavy bug infestations. I once took roach motels to Jamaica on a mission trip. The floors moved. The bedspreads moved. The roaches were too big to squeeze through the doors of roach hotels. I needed hand grenades. I considered it a blessing when a member of my party had to be rushed back to the States after the first day for open-heart surgery. The surgery needed for life was received. This was fantastic. I was rescued from roach guerilla warfare. Elated I'd been "saved," what can I say? Surely know I told God, "Thank you."

The next time, I'd request Russia and cold weather. Maybe the roaches wouldn't be so bad and I wouldn't have to sweat, physically or mentally. *God, you knew I was weak. Roaches can live up to a month with their heads cut off. Was it really necessary to create them?*

Who am I to question God and yet, I still chase after him.

Sometimes I cry, "God, can you confide in me like you did Abraham? Can you tell me what you're going to do? You warned him about Sodom and

Gomorrah. You even let him respectfully dicker with you about how many people you would save."

But sometimes, God says nothing. He's not in the wind. He's not in the earthquake. He's not in the fire. And that still small voice is so still and small, I strain to hear something and say, "Well, God, if you're not saying anything today guess I'm on vacation too."

I dig through the scriptures searching for His will like a dog searching for last week's buried bone thinking, "I knew where it was last week. I'm on the right trail. I thought I'd remember right where I was supposed to go." Wasn't there a verse in there about love?

But right when I think I have everything figured out, I realize I know nothing at all. God teases with new knowledge and allows me to be tested with new trials as he searches my sometimes-rebellious heart to find from what metal I am forged.

And the refining process was and still is grueling.

Though he let me know my child was going to have a horrendous car wreck, he didn't let me know the outcome. I sweated out those few days until the doomed day arrived, totally trusting in him, though not knowing if he was calling my child home or if she would be maimed for life. But I trusted because I had no other choice, really. Wailing and gnashing of teeth had never been my style. I'm the more stoic stomach-ulcer type.

My child climbed out of a totaled car with a few scratches, which was a lot better than my nerve-wracked body could confess.

God, did you think I would look good wearing hip plastic?

You do know the difference between colostomy bags and Chanel off the shoulder?

And, yes, God does have a sense of humor because he said I was created in his own image and he did visit earth in the form of Jesus. So he had to know what I was talking about. "And being in anguish, he prayed more earnestly, and his sweat was like drops of blood falling to the ground." (Luke 22:44 NLT)

Yes, he knew. And he knows.

He knows.

But sometimes he's not talking.

Or is it I who am not listening?

It's just that sometimes God, to get whatever it was you wanted me to do, done I needed an email, a phone call, or handwriting on the wall that said something other than *mene, mene, tekel, parsin* (which if Daniel had interpreted in plain Southern slang would have been, "Looks like you're gonna die!")

But even when I didn't hear a thing but the wind, I could look outside and know he was there because of the flaming sunsets, the brilliant lilies clothed so majestically, my raspberry parfait peonies bowing down in worship in my garden, the loving animals and the beautiful family, I'd been blessed to share a life with.

Yes, God, you were there.

You're here now.

Even when you're not talking you're speaking through sign language.

Art language.

Beautiful music orchestrated by your hand while the Tufted Titmouse calls "Peter, Peter, Peter," to remind me upon what rock you built your church.

And if I believe what you said, because your Word tells us you cannot lie, then I have to believe that Jesus is the same yesterday, today, and tomorrow. Then I have to also believe miracles do still happen.

You proved that to me the night three doctors told me Daddy would die. But again, I cried out to you even louder and harder until, like the deer, I panted for your Living Water. Daddy miraculously lived. The doctors couldn't save him — couldn't understand how he was saved — but my almighty God could get the job done because I asked it of him.

You heard me. You hear me now though you don't always answer with a yes.

You were and are always there and in everything — waiting for me to recognize you, acknowledge you, to turn around and return to you when I lapse.

If only I'd reached out to call on God more when I was in my youth.

Yes, there are regrets because I didn't trust him enough, thought I could do everything myself. The past, however, is the past, and in the future, I will be forever and ever, chasing God.

Vicki H. Moss

15
Beauty from Ashes

Carlos Rios awoke on Thanksgiving Day, 1994, thankful for all he had. On this warm November morning, Genie, his wife of seven and a half years, lay beside him. Snuggled together across the hall slept his two dark-eyed, sweet-faced daughters: Ana, five, and Raquel, almost two. For three years, they had lived in Todos Santos, a small Mexican town on the Baja peninsula. The Evangelical Alliance Mission (TEAM) had sent them there with one other couple to establish a church. When they arrived, Carlos, a native Colombian, and Genie, a South Carolinian, found the area steeped in voodoo and superstition. Only recently had they begun to see progress, and for that Carlos was thankful.

The day promised to be unforgettable. The two missionary couples planned to drive an hour across the peninsula to the neighboring town of San Jose to share Thanksgiving dinner with four other missionary families. Only one concern niggled at the edge of Carlos's happiness that morning.

Genie had been experiencing migraine-like headaches and high blood pressure for several days. Medicine from the local pharmacy had little effect. All night long Genie had tossed restlessly beside him, moaning occasionally in her sleep. He hoped she had rested enough to be able to enjoy the festivities of the day.

As the morning progressed, Genie's condition deteriorated. Carlos knew she wasn't well enough to travel. Not wanting the girls to miss the celebration, he sent them to San Jose with the other missionary family. By 10:00 A.M. Genie was fading in and out of consciousness, and he knew he had to take her to the nearest hospital, more than an hour away.

Upon their arrival, doctors rushed to examine her and performed a battery of tests. Genie's breathing became more labored, and her body convulsed from a steadily climbing fever. A spinal tap revealed the cause of her illness — Spinal Meningitis.

As they began intravenous antibiotics, her doctor spoke words Carlos never expected to hear. "It may be too late. Even if she responds to the antibiotics, she could have brain damage and be a vegetable for the rest of her life."

Forbidden to enter the intensive care unit, Carlos paced the halls crying out to God. *Genie is leaving me*, he realized. As he pictured his wife's sweet face, he remembered the Bible verse they had been memorizing with their young daughters. "Never will I leave you. Never will I forsake you." (Hebrews 13:5 NIV) It was if God had His hand on Carlos' shoulder and was saying, "I am with you."

Genie died two hours later.

The next month passed in a whirl of funeral arrangements, memorial services, and travel. In quiet moments, Carlos' mind bounced from one frightening question to the next. *What is going to happen to us? To the girls? To the ministry?*

Carlos and his daughters traveled to Wheaton, Illinois, where Genie's parents lived. Gene and Bev Tindall worked at the national headquarters of the TEAM ministry and lived in an apartment on the grounds. They knew that Carlos, as a TEAM missionary, would be able to meet with a nearby counselor to help him work through the grieving process. They turned their study into a bedroom for Carlos and outfitted another room with bunk beds for the girls. "You are a part of our family," Bev said, "and if you want to stay with us, you are more than welcome."

At night, when the house was quiet and the girls were asleep, Bev could hear Carlos crying. "I miss Genie so much," Carlos would say. Although grieving the loss of her daughter, she knew his loss was greater. He had lost not only his wife and the mother of his children, but his best friend.

In the days that followed, Bev comforted her granddaughters. They enjoyed strolls through the neighborhood, and as they focused on God's creation, their conversation often turned to prayer. Bev and Ana specifically prayed for a new mommy.

Six thousand miles away, God was answering those prayers.

Sandy Morse, also a TEAM missionary, was attending a monthly Prayer Day in Tokyo, Japan. During the prayer time, one of the missionaries shared the tragic story of Carlos and his family.

"I prayed out loud for them," remembers Sandy. "I had no idea who they were, but I felt an overwhelming burden to pray for those little girls and this guy." She didn't think of them again.

The ministry Sandy was working with began to fall apart, and her workload became overwhelming. Her personal life followed suit. She was engaged to a navy chaplain, but realized she'd sought the relationship out of loneliness, not love. She broke off her engagement and slipped into a deep depression. As she made plans to leave Japan and return home to seek counseling, the mission organization directed her to Wheaton, where she moved into in a small apartment next door to TEAM staff members Gene and Bev Tindall.

Sandy was in and out of the TEAM office and began to develop a friendship with the woman who worked there. Sandy remembers, "Bev was friendly, smiling, incredibly helpful, and always laughing." Bev invited Sandy to attend her church, and their friendship deepened.

After having Gene and Bev over for a dinner of meatloaf and mashed potatoes, Sandy discovered the mixer she'd borrowed from Bev earlier in the day. She carried it to the Tindall's apartment and knocked on their door. Carlos answered and invited her in. *Whoa*, was Sandy's unspoken response as she looked into Carlos's warm brown eyes. She felt an immediate attraction to the handsome Latin man with such gentle ways. Surprised and flustered, she delivered the mixture and quickly left.

After several months of intensive counseling, Sandy was able to work through her ministry and personal struggles and gain peace and perspective. As she continued to heal, Sandy began to pray about where God would send her next. She loved church planting, but had concluded Japan was too hard for a single woman. TEAM leaders told her of the ministry in Mexico and suggested she take an exploratory trip to visit the area and meet the team.

Before she left, Bev and Gene Tindall planned a big birthday party for Sandy. Carlos and his girls were on the guest list. After the party, several of the singles decided to go play miniature golf, and Carlos and Sandy went along. In between putts, Sandy shared about her upcoming trip to Mexico and her need to brush up on her high school Spanish.

"I can help you with that," Carlos offered, and they began meeting together. As they shared details about their past, they discovered they had attended Columbia Bible College in Columbia, South Carolina, at the same time. Because Sandy was in the seminary, and Carlos and Genie were in the undergraduate program, they had never met.

As Carlos healed emotionally, he was again able to participate in ministry. He volunteered in a Hispanic church, and Sandy began attending with him. When she left for Mexico, he shyly pressed a note into her hand. Sandy recalls, "It was the first indication that there was anything more than friendship on his mind."

Meanwhile, Carlos had been reflecting on the wise words of his grief counselor. During one of the sessions he said, "You know, maybe God will bring a new love into your life and into the lives of your daughters."

"Oh no," Carlos responded, "That's not possible. There's no room in my heart to love someone else."

"God can make room," his counselor said.

Sandy returned from her trip to Mexico, confident that God was leading her to serve there. Things were also moving ahead in her relationship with Carlos. They were spending more time together, and their relationship was growing deeper. Through the time they spent together, God was healing their hearts.

One night, before heading to dinner at a Mexican restaurant, Sandy noticed the girls seemed especially excited. As Carlos kissed them goodbye, Ana sang out, "Papi, don't forget the R-E-N-G!"

Yes, this was the night. In the quiet of the restaurant, Carlos pulled out a pair of Ana's heart-shaped sunglasses and put them on his face, now lit up with a boyish grin. Then he asked Sandy to marry him.

"I can't even see your eyes," Sandy shrieked with joy and laughter. "How can I tell you yes or no?!"

They were married five months later with Ana and Raquel as their beaming flower girls. Surrounded by family, church friends, and fellow missionaries, four-year-old Raquel's little heart overflowed with happiness as she pronounced, "We're all getting married!"

Everyone agreed that the marriage was the answer to their prayers. God had made new room in both Sandy's and Carlos' hearts — a place for a love He had designed for them from the beginning of time, a love planted during life's pain and heartaches, but one that would blossom as they worked together as a family and a team in Mexico.

Lori Hatcher

16

Easily Entertained

Momma took a sip of coffee and began to giggle.

"What?" I asked with a smile.

"I just had this memory about you when you were little," she said as she reached over and touched my hand. Then, she started a belly laugh.

"What in the world? Don't keep me in suspense!"

"Alright, alright." She gasped for air. "Since you could walk you had a habit of following me around, yanking on my skirt and asking, 'What can I do now, Momma?'"

I laughed. "You know, I vaguely remember that."

"You wore me out with that question. I'd give you an idea, and off you'd go, but you'd always come back. So one day, I remember like it was yesterday, I was making spaghetti sauce, and you came into the kitchen, all pouty, and I knew you were about to ask *that* question. I had to do something to save you from yourself, so I turned off the stove, grabbed your little hands in mine and sat down with you on the kitchen floor.

"'Now, Kay,' I said, 'I want you to listen to me. I'm going to tell you a secret. It's very important. Do you understand?' Your tiny curls bobbed up and down. 'I could give you lots of fun things to do right now. I have lots of ideas. We've got a big yard. You have a playhouse out there, and upstairs there's a room filled with all sorts toys and stuff to make things — paper and crayons, ribbons and fabric and glue, but, you know what, if I keep giving you things to do you'll never learn how to entertain yourself, and that's one of the most important things there is in the whole wide world — to be able to entertain yourself.

"'So, from now on let's see what kind of play ideas you can come up with on your own. Find out what you like to do and do it! You don't need me to tell you. Why, you're going on five-years-old. You're a big girl now! How 'bout you try playing on your own. OK?'"

"I sent you on your way, and that was the end of your skirt-yanking days. Once I gave you permission to discover your own interests, you never again asked me, 'What can a do now, Momma?'"

A couple of years later Daddy took over another phase of this entertain-yourself education. Every summer our family took a vacation. One year my brothers and I had a snowball fight in July on top of Colorado's Pike's Peak. Another year we witnessed a mountain goat standing high up in George Washington's eye on Mount Rushmore in South Dakota! On still another trip we rode on the backs of giant turtles in Oklahoma. But no matter where our final destination happened to be, we almost always started our trips with a visit to Chicago. It was Momma's hometown and she had a sister there. It was also my parents' city of romance since they had met while Daddy was stationed there during World War II, courted and married there.

What an exhilarating city — especially for kids from the country! And nowhere was that excitement more pronounced for me than at the multi-leveled, ever-showering Buckingham Fountain, in Grant Park — the vast expanse of green nestled between Chicago's bustling Michigan Avenue and its watery border, Lake Michigan.

During our stay we would always have one day where we split-up. Momma would be off to Marshall Field's department store to study the latest fashions and bring back one of her favorites treats — Frango Mints. My brothers would have a special play-day with our all-boy cousins and Daddy and I would drive downtown to Buckingham Fountain to share our favorite pastime: watching people and making up stories about them.

Daddy could be amazingly accurate. Like the time he said, "See that man over there — the one with the white hair, standing next to the fountain wall?" He paused, giving me time to spy the guy.

"Got him," I said as I locked him in my view.

"You probably can't see it right now. He's standing in front of it, but a minute ago I saw a pink rose lying on the wall behind him."

As the man shifted, I saw it, too. "Yes, I see it!"

"I'll bet he's waiting for his high school sweetheart. They married other people a long time ago and have been separated for many years. But his wife and her husband have died now, and they've decided to meet because, secretly, they never stopped being sweet on each other."

I threw in, "And earlier, when they talked on the phone, she told him she'd be wearing a pink dress. That's why his rose is pink!" We laughed and waited as we looked around for new stories.

Sure enough, ten minutes later, an older woman in a pale pink dress with silver hair tied up in a neat bun entered the fountain area. When the man saw her coming, he picked up the rose and began to move quickly toward her. When they finally met they stood for several seconds staring at one another. Then, they held hands and talked for a few more minutes before falling into each other's arms.

Daddy laughed and slapped his knee. "What did I tell you? And lookee there, she's got on a pink dress — just like you said!"

Some of our stories were short, some went on for hours, but all were affectionate homespun creations that kept us entertained. People watching and making up stories became a way of life — one that has delivered delight even in times of stress and discomfort.

I can think of no greater gift a parent can give to a child than the ability and the desire, no, the passion to be so engaged in life that being bored simply doesn't register to them. My parents gave me their love for life and helped me create my own. With lessons that have lasted for more than sixty years, I am grateful for the love of Momma and Daddy. They lovingly raised three children, and there's not a bored bone in any of our bodies!

With all the things in this world to see, hear, taste, touch, feel, smell and do — pray, think, read, write, sing, say, build, play, drive, ride, dream, fill in the blank, how is it possible to be bored? Perhaps the true gift is in knowing there is always a choice.

Kay Harper

17

All It Takes Is a Baby

A ll it takes is a baby to change one's life.

The chirping of my cell phone interrupted the next round of play in the card game my husband and I were enjoying with some friends one November evening. My daughter-in-law, Lisa, started telling me about a Christmas ornament she had bought for their tree by describing an adorable bear holding some small shoes.

Well, that's cute but why is she telling me now? She usually sent pictures of the two of them decorating their tree instead of calling me about it. It took me a few moments to realize the bear on the ornament she was describing was pregnant. This had been her way of telling our son, Kenny, he was a father-to-be.

Comprehension finally made the trek to my brain and I said, "You mean you really are?"

As the months passed we kept up with the baby's progress and found out we were having a girl. I immediately started buying pink — pink blankets, pink ribbons and bows, pink shoes. You get the picture. I was already basking in the grandmother aura.

We knew ahead of time the birth would be by C-section and as the due date approached, delivery was scheduled. However, little Keira had other plans. A week before the surgery, Lisa visited the doctor and was immediately sent to the hospital. We got the call early in the morning and our other son and I left right away to travel to Florida. My husband was away with his job so we kept him updated on the progress.

About halfway into our seven-hour trip, Kenny called and announced, "She's here." Keira Lynn Latta entered the world with a head full of black hair, liquid blue eyes and weighing in at ten pounds, five ounces.

Lisa had been diagnosed with gestational diabetes late in the pregnancy and medication had been dispensed; but because of the drugs Lisa had been on to lower her blood sugar, the baby's levels were now below normal. Keira was moved to Newborn Intensive Care Unit and administered an IV through an umbilical feed. We visited her several times a day since she couldn't occupy Mom's room.

Lisa's difficulties were just beginning. The C-section, diabetes, and now anemia required Lisa stay longer at the hospital than Keira. Kenny and I took the baby home amid tears from Mom. My heart felt for her. No one wants to stay in the hospital while their infant leaves without them. Many parents have to leave their babies in the hospital for days, weeks, or months after the mother goes home. Our situation was the opposite.

I enjoyed being MiMi to Keira her first night at home even though I had to adjust to waking at wee hours of the morning for diaper changes and feedings. After all, it had been a long time.

Lisa came home a couple of days later, just in time to make the graduation ceremony at the school she had been attending to get her Medical Assistant degree. I was amazed she was able to march in and go on stage to receive her diploma. But later that night another scare crawled in, when she started retaining fluid, experiencing severe pain, and having difficulty breathing.

Kenny rushed her to the ER at the closest hospital, near where he worked as a Nuclear Medical Technician. While Lisa spent five days in the hospital, Kenny and I took Keira to see her every day. Finally, release day came and the family was whole again at home.

An indescribable feeling of love made my heart swell holding that precious bundle for the first time. I never thought I could love another human being as much as I do my own children, but when our children have their own children, the feeling is multiplied as if my own babies are combined into another bundle. Maybe it's because I have learned from the mistakes made with my kids that I can now relax and have fun. Joy overflows for these descendants of our flesh.

Because we are now separated by several hours from our new granddaughter, our travel schedules revolve around ways to spend time with her. Shopping has changed too, because I want to buy so many things I see for little girls.

Talking about her and sharing pictures with others, whether they want to see them or not, is an obsession I have acquired since Keira's birth.

Over two thousand years ago another mother found out she was going to have a baby. She experienced difficulties also, but of a different kind than Keira's mother did.

Mary must have been afraid. As her body's signs indicated to others that she had sinned to become pregnant while not married, thoughts of the law's requirements about being stoned must have gone through that young girl's mind. After the angel appeared to Joseph and told him of the impending holy birth, the couple still faced the ridicule of their peers. A difficult journey for the census and to pay taxes awaited them.

But on that starry night in Bethlehem, wonderful love came to earth wrapped in a bundle of human flesh. That was Deity in a newborn. He was love, is love, and he taught us to love. The newborn became the Lamb upon the altar of judgment and the ugliness of sin was conquered. He was the only baby who has ever been born whose destiny was to die so we can have abundant life and know the fullness of God's love.

Barbara Latta

Figlia Bella

Don't depend on things like fancy hairdos or gold jewelry
or expensive clothes to make you look beautiful.
Be beautiful in your heart by being gentle and quiet.
This kind of beauty will last, and God considers it very special.

1 Peter 3:3-4 (CEV)

Figlia Bella!" Fifty plus years later, I still hear the endearing words echo. *Figlia bella*, Italian for "beautiful daughter" was the way my grandmother referred to me.

In today's society, "beautiful" has unusual standards. With one gaze at magazine covers while we wait at a checkout lane, we question our personal attractiveness. Models and mannequins remind us that we will never have their look. Persuasive diet and exercise plans tell us by nature of their advertisement that we are "less than," and challenge us to improve our appearance.

I was not a particularly beautiful girl — in fact I was chubby — and I often wore my cousin's hand me downs, but in my grandmother's eyes I was beautiful.

Society's standards of beauty differ from God's. He values our heart and our character. He sees us through the eyes of love. Apparently, my grandmother did too.

Father, help me not to adopt the patterns of the world when it comes to assessing beauty — my own or others' — but to see beauty by your standards. Amen

Marilyn Nutter

Because I Love Him

Sixty-three is too young to have dementia, and Dandy-Walker Syndrome is too uncommon to affect my husband. Yet, the reality is Doug has both. He was born with Dandy-Walker, a condition which involves hydrocephalus in the lower back part of the brain and also frequently includes other conditions, such as dementia, melanosis, breathing abnormalities and psychosis. He managed to excel throughout life while it remained undetected.

His mother seemingly never noticed the delays in his development and continued to push him until his achievements surpassed those of his twin sister. It wasn't until about five years ago, when we noticed significant deterioration in Doug's ability to walk and work at overhead tasks, that a skilled neurologist made Doug's Dandy-Walker diagnosis.

Doug has so many lovable qualities it would have been impossible for me to say "No" when he asked me to marry him in 1996. We were both in our late forties. Each of us had a difficult first marriage and had been single parenting for several years. Not wanting to repeat our past mistakes, we dated for two and a half years before deciding to wed.

I liked the fact that our backgrounds were similar. Both of our fathers were grocers, our mothers had been telephone operators. We each had only one female sibling. Each of us had adopted children. We attained the same levels of education — a bachelor's degree and some post grad work. Doug and I shared the same religious beliefs.

In my first marriage, my husband was not a good reader or speller. Doug's literary skills were excellent. I soon began to depend on him to edit my writing before I sent it to a publisher.

Doug had worked many years as a tax auditor for the state. Unlike my past experience, with a husband who jumped from job to job and moved from house to house while accruing debt, Doug had carefully planned for his financial future, building up a generous retirement package and home equity. For the first time in my life, I knew I was in a reciprocal love relationship.

One of the major issues for me, before I agreed to marry Doug, was my birthday. In my past life, my husband of twenty-four years never once remembered my birthday. I was not subtle about its approach. I started a birthday countdown six months in advance. Still, my husband could not even bother to acknowledge the day. I was not about to marry anyone else who was so complacent about my birthday. So Doug and I talked this out early in our courtship. He rose to the occasion every year, making sure my birthdays were special celebrations that honored my life, including activities and people who meant the most to me.

I began to notice small signs of dementia. Doug could not find the car in the parking lot or he could not find his cap sitting in plain sight on the counter where he always placed it. His frustration looking for these "lost" items climbed to a new level. I read fear or anger in his eyes.

He tried to do tasks we had just completed, like paying the bills. I felt a need to have constant oversight of the business activities of managing a household — things Doug had always done so efficiently. In spite of wearing a watch and having calendars and clocks all over the house, Doug would ask me every ten minutes what time or day it was. He misreported conversations he had with family and friends and swore that his version was truth.

One day I asked Doug to edit a piece of my writing prior to submitting it. "I'm making a couple of changes," he said. "I'm just putting some punctuation inside the quotation marks."

Trusting him, I said, "Okay."

But when I reread it, his change was obviously incorrect.

I tried to discuss it with him. He was adamant. I finally agreed, but changed it back the way I had it originally.

My birthday was a few weeks after the episode with the punctuation. We made plans to attend a local sausage and kraut festival. Just as we were preparing to leave the house a family member phoned. Doug told them we were on our way to celebrate my son's birthday. I knew then my reign as party princess was over. He was no longer able to honor the one thing that had been most important, the pledge he had made and so faithfully kept all those years of marriage.

If I did not love Doug, the loss of his cherished attributes could have destroyed our marriage. Neither of us, despite our track records, believes in divorce. We married "for better or for worse." Dementia and Dandy-Walker Syndrome were not a part of our long-range plans. They affected us way sooner than we think is fair.

Doug wakes me up every ten to twelve minutes during the night and asks me to take him to the bathroom. He forgets he has just been. He is unable to walk there on his own. I take him.

Sometimes, love does not sleep.

Then I remember the scripture in 1 Corinthians 13:4-8 NIV:

Love is patient, love is kind.

It does not envy, it does not boast, it is not proud.

It is not rude, it is not self-seeking,

it is not easily angered, it keeps no record of wrongs.

Love does not delight in evil but rejoices with the truth.

It always protects, always trusts, always hopes, always perseveres.

Love never fails.

Mason K Brown

20

Babe

B abe's name completely fit her high-maintenance personality.
She was a remarkably gorgeous Treeing Walker Coonhound, with lines and coloration so perfect that she won her first competition at the age of ten months. She came from a long line of champions known not only for their perfect physical condition, but for their extremely superior intelligence and their distinct, much-louder-than-normal bay.

When my husband told me he wanted that breed of dog, I researched all the information I could find about them. Despite my extensive efforts, nothing prepared me for what I would experience with this new member of our family.

Babe was incredibly intelligent — frighteningly so. My husband could look at her, tell her in a normal tone of voice that he wanted her to watch over our children, and she would immediately go and sit next to them, watching over them like a fiercely protective mama.

The breeder warned that she could open doors by using her paws to turn the knobs. I didn't believe it until I watched that take place.

Whenever the contractor we had hired to do some work on our old farmhouse came to do his work, we had to lock Babe away because she would bare her teeth at him as she snarled with a particularly threatening throaty growl. Although we initially could not figure out why Babe had taken a particular dislike to the man, we later discovered that she had a better sense of character than we did. We learned we were only one of many families in the region who had been ripped off by the contractor through shoddy and faulty workmanship as well as cheating each of us out of tens of thousands of dollars.

I sometimes wish that I had let her bite a chunk out of him.

My husband loved Babe and the dog wholeheartedly returned his love. Unfortunately, that did not bode as well for me, the rival female for my husband's affections. Babe made her great displeasure of me known through occasional defecations on my pillow, the carefully selective destruction of my favorite shoes, and urination on my favorite blanket. She also regularly slithered under the sheets on my side of the bed, using her teeth to pull the blanket up and over her body, so that when I tried to get into bed at night, I was met with the steely-eyed stare of my husband's other babe.

She also liked to mess with the other animals of the household, making sure they knew who their boss was (and no, it was not me). Many times, I had to run outside to rescue some poor chicken or duck from Babe's energetic pursuit. Sometimes I could corral the poor, frightened fowl back to the safety of their enclosure, somehow opened by Babe. Other times, I would be chased around the yard as I tried to hold the delighted dog off with one hand while tightly grasping an upside-down fowl in my other hand, away from her snapping jaws.

We lived on the corner of two roads, so my neighbors regularly observed (with great glee) my gymnastics. I am still known as The-Lady-Who-Runs-In-Circles.

Babe had an affinity for stealing food off kitchen counters, so at Thanksgiving wails of despair were often heard as another twenty-plus pound turkey made its way down the happy dog's gullet. She also liked chocolate chip cookies; despite the fact that she had eaten several trays' worth of them at one sitting, she never learned her lesson from getting sick.

Despite our competitive relationship, I loved that dog fiercely, especially when she protected me in my husband's absence. When he left for combat after joining the military the day after 9/11, some thugs broke into the house. I was living with two small children, in a rural town far away from the safety of law enforcement. Babe provided us with needed protection.

I can't begin to recount just how many nights I awakened with her standing protectively over me, growling at someone trying to get into the house. One night when I could hear people on the other side of the front door, Babe's loud barking was what caused them to take off in a peal of scorched rubber and smoke. When people trespassed on our property and behaved in a threatening way, Babe's snapping set of teeth initiated their hasty departure.

When my daughter awakened at night, crying from missing her daddy who was fighting overseas, Babe would quietly move to her side, refusing to leave until my daughter fell asleep again.

When my husband returned home, Babe's joyous bays and frantic licks on my husband's face brought tears to my eyes, as this loyal and fierce dog welcomed her favorite human home.

I did not think that I would cry much when she passed away, because she was not my dog, but when she died in her favorite place — my husband's lap — I bawled until I had no more tears to shed.

I miss Babe. There isn't a day that goes by when I do not think of her, the beautiful dog who made my blood pressure soar, but who also lovingly protected my children and me when her favorite human was not there to do so.

Marybeth Mitcham

21

Porch Light Curfew

Click! The porch light flashed one last time. The prim, white-haired dorm mom had given her final warning and the young ladies scurried inside. Girls in the small Christian college I attended in the 1950s knew enough to get through that imposing front door before Mom G turned the key and locked up for the night.

Most of the boyfriends, banished by the 10:00 P.M. curfew, returned to their dormitories. With romance over for the evening, students deserted the darkened porch until morning.

Those of us without dates lounged in our rooms playing cards or studying. My roommate's boyfriend came from their hometown for the weekend as often as he could. Early in our freshman year, they shared one last goodnight kiss at the warning light, and he started home. The events of that four-hour drive would bring romance into my life.

Traffic on the Missouri roads was light in the middle of the night, and my roommate's boyfriend had a lonely trip from Fayette back to El Dorado Springs. As he neared his destination, his eyelids grew heavier and heavier. When he could no longer fight off the drowsiness, he drifted off to sleep and ran off the road.

He awoke uninjured, but the incident alarmed his family. They knew he wouldn't give up the weekend visits to his girlfriend, but the possibility of a serious accident called for precautions to keep him awake.

The safety measure he took was to invite Bud, his single brother, to come along and keep him company. That meant his girlfriend — my roommate — had the job of finding somebody to entertain Bud. She talked me into a blind date. I agreed to go but with apprehension. I didn't know anything about Bud, except what my roommate told me.

She said he had had a serious girlfriend in high school, and he was quiet. How would I, a shy, first-year college student without much dating experience, get through a weekend with an equally shy and quiet stranger?

The brothers arrived on Saturday afternoon and checked in at the hotel in the small rural town. They rented a room on the second floor. One bathroom down the hallway served all the hotel guests. Although not fancy, it had the necessary equipment, including one bathtub.

My roommate and I waited anxiously in our fourth-floor dorm room until the telephone in the hallway rang. Another girl answered and yelled, "Ruth Pentecost and LeAnn Foster, your dates have arrived." We made our way down the four flights of stairs, Ruth in eager anticipation and me a bit shaky in the knees.

Our dates sat in the parlor watching the snowy screen of a black-and-white television — the only one in the dorm. I smiled at the nice-looking young man, who had dark hair combed straight back, and beautiful brown eyes. Even without the good looks, I'm sure his aftershave would have won me over. He smelled so good!

After introductions, the four of us set out for our first evening together. We bought hot dogs and buns and drove to the city park for a picnic. We enjoyed the beautiful October evening, walked in the crunchy fallen leaves, and talked beside the lake after we'd eaten. I laughed at Bud's corny jokes, and our initial nervousness passed.

Bud's brother told him ahead of time one of our weekend activities would be church attendance. Bud had never been to church. In preparation, he spent part of his monthly paycheck on appropriate clothes. The brothers arrived at the dorm parlor Sunday morning dressed for church. Bud was trim and handsome in a nice gray suit — the first he'd ever owned.

They couldn't make the trip every weekend but came as often as they could. With just one car for the four of us, every visit became a double date. Then at the end of our freshman year, our weekends as a foursome ended. My roommate went home to marry her boyfriend.

Although Bud didn't have his brother to come along to keep him company the next year, he continued to make the four-hour drive. Mom G still stood by the door and flicked the light switch, giving the nightly ten o'clock curfew warning to young ladies and their dates.

Our weekends together were still infrequent, about one every month. We'd take drives, sometimes going to Jefferson City to see the state capitol. Each time he came, Bud brought his suit and went to church with me on Sunday morning.

We filled the days between visits with letters and an occasional phone call. When he called, someone would answer our fourth-floor wall phone and call out, "LeAnn Foster, you have a phone call." We didn't talk long, because Bud had to keep pushing coins into a pay phone or we'd be cut off.

By the time we'd dated for about a year, he asked me to marry him. This made me as nervous as the prospect of our first meeting. I wanted to say yes, but marriage is so serious and I didn't want to risk making a mistake. Being persistent, he asked again. This time I gave the right answer. My friends celebrated my engagement in our dorm way — they filled our fourth-floor bathtub with water and threw me in.

After a year of dating as a twosome, Bud and I said our last goodbye under the flickering light. We whispered about the plans we'd made. The light switch clicked, and I hurried inside. With a quick backward look, I watched Bud walk down the steps and head to his car. In two weeks, we would be together again, for the rest of our lives.

To prepare for our wedding, Mother and I went to our farm pasture and picked Shasta daisies. We put food coloring in glasses of water and stuck the stems in the glasses to produce the colored petals we wanted. Mother baked the wedding cake ahead of time. The night before the wedding my dorm friends, who had come to be my bridesmaids and musicians, decorated the cake. While we worked in the kitchen, the men sat in the living room and played cards.

On a warm June afternoon, my friends helped me into the satin bridal gown Mother had made. Dad escorted me down the aisle, where Bud waited in his gray suit. That suit became an important part of his wardrobe for several years, for he wore it many Sundays as he not only attended church but also became a Sunday school teacher and elder.

My former roommate, who is now my sister-in-law, loves to tell how she set up my husband and me on a blind date that led to our marriage. It's been more than sixty years since the four of us stood on that well-lit dorm porch, dreading the click of the light switch.

Our first weekend together started as a precaution to keep Bud's brother safe on the road. But by our second foursome date, clearly an intentional plan grew to keep us together — a plan we've never regretted.

LeAnn Campbell

22

Moment of Love

I experienced unexpected tragedy a few years back. After a minor surgery I began to hemorrhage. Ten transfusions saved my life but I needed to be put on life support to keep my breathing stable. My family rushed from around the U.S. to my bedside.

I remained on life support for ten days. During that time I developed sepsis pneumonia and my prognosis was uncertain.

As prayers were lifted up from my church and other churches around the country, I began to improve.

One of my coworkers had the idea to get a guest book for people to write down their thoughts to me while I was on life support. Fifteen days later I awoke to notes of love, scriptures of healing, and encouragement.

I was overwhelmed with the love expressed by family, coworkers, and brothers and sisters in Christ. I read it several times, each time tears and emotion overwhelmed me. My twenty-one-year-old son also had written in the book.

As many Moms and sons do, we had our moments of disagreement. But I knew he loved me. My son has a mild version of Aspergers and he didn't often express this love in writing. He rarely sent birthday or Mother's Day cards. He did give great hugs and said, "I love you" as he said goodnight or goodbye.

I learned later that he never left my bedside during those ten days. He told his employer that he would not return to work until I was off life support. However, nothing meant more to me than the words written in that small black book. During those days my face had been swollen beyond recognition. The IVs of water that had sustained my life had changed every inch of my appearance. Even so, a few days before I was taken off of the respirator my son wrote:

> Mom, today someone said something, and I saw you make that
> face where you squint your eyebrows like you do when you

don't understand something. I knew then you were in there, when I saw that expression, and that God had answered my prayers. I knew you were going to be okay. Mom, I miss you and I LOVE YOU! I can't wait for you to come home with me.

As a single mom, I never felt so loved by my only son. Those words are forever etched in my mind. Not only the words, but that in my darkest hours, my son saw me and knew that I was there. It was like God tapped him on the shoulder and said, "I've heard your prayer. Your mom will be okay soon."

I thank God that through that experience I will always have those words, and that my son will always know God answers prayers.

Dorothy Floyd

23

Desiring God: Hubba-Hubba Love

The whole week was filled with candy hearts and Valentine's Day wishes. How opportune that our Sunday school class conversation centered on desiring God — a desire for more of God that tips over into hunger, thirst, and a longing to be with him all the time. In an attempt to make it relevant, our teacher asked, "What did you think when you first saw your spouse?"

My response was automatic. I didn't have to think about it all. Out it came in the middle of Sunday school, "Hubba-hubba!"

John and I have been married for almost thirty-six years and I can still say that he causes me to think, *hubba-hubba* every time I see him. He is my best friend. My soulmate. My hubba-hubba love, not just on Valentine's Day, but every day.

Desiring God — A Thirst for More

That whole face-flaming moment came about as we discussed the love that the Psalmist desired for God. Psalm 63 NASB says,

> O God, You are my God; I shall seek You earnestly;
> My soul thirsts for You, my flesh yearns for You,
> In a dry and weary land where there is no water.

That word *earnestly*, means *early.* It means I will seek God first. I will seek him diligently.

Psalm 42:1-2 NASB says,

> As the deer pants for the water brooks,
> so my soul pants for You, O God.
> My soul thirsts for God, for the living God.

The root for this word *pants* means to long for. And "my soul *thirsts* for God" means *to suffer thirst* — an incredible thirst longing to be satisfied.

In our further discussion in class about a desire for God, we talked about the hunger of an addict. All they can think about is that *one thing*. This is the essence of the yearning we should experience for God. This is a hubba-hubba love story — a call from the Beloved to his beloved.

The Enemy Hates Our Desiring God

The enemy of our soul would like to distract us and replace that longing with a longing for something cheap and unsatisfying. We see this happening in the world. Love is given to cheap imitations. Hunger and thirst seek to be satiated from a cloudy well. And our worth is like a needy child scrambling for scraps.

But, when we see Jesus for who he is, we become overcome by a hubba-hubba moment that calls us to a deeper relationship — a place where we are filled rather than depleted. When our Beloved calls our name and draws us to himself, he wraps us in pure love and grace. And, in that moment we discover what we have missed. We find what we have been longing for. And, our hubba-hubba love sets us on a path of knowing the One who knows us best.

God provides what we hunger for: pure love, extravagant grace, and a place called home.

Jeanne Doyon

24
Instilling Confidence

My seven-year-old son burst into sobs as he handed me a test paper with an F written in red ink at the top. "The other kids said you'd be mad at me when you saw the F."

I looked into my little boy's shame-filled blue eyes and wrapped my arms around him. "Well, they're wrong because I'm not mad at all, honey."

Justin drew his head back, tears streaming down his face. "But I failed, Mommy. I got an F. And I'm the only one in the class who flunked the test."

"There's no reason to be upset." Smiling, I stroked his face. "An F is actually a very good grade."

Justin sniffled. "It is?"

"Yes, it is. You see, an A tells us what you do know and an F tells us what you don't know." I wiped the dampness from his cheeks. "Always remember this: an F is actually a very good grade because it tells us what we need to work on."

His lower lip quivered. "Some of the kids made fun of me."

"Well, the next time they make fun of you because they think you got a bad grade, you tell them that your mom said an F is actually a very good grade."

The corners of Justin's mouth rose.

"Let's go out to the kitchen. While you have a snack, I'll look over the test and once I figure out what you don't know, I'll teach it to you."

Justin munched on apple slices as I scrutinized the test. Although I had stopped teaching professionally when my son was born, my educational skills were put to daily use with my own children. I analyzed Justin's answers and formed a plan to teach him the things he didn't understand each day after school. I knew exactly what to do and what to say because I, too, had failed in a subject, been ridiculed, and thought myself stupid for many years.

At the beginning of my junior year at Penn State University, my academic advisor reviewed my transcript. "You haven't taken any math classes yet," he observed.

My stomach sickened. "Can I substitute another subject for math?"

"No," he said, shaking his head. "In order to graduate, you're required to take one math and two statistics classes. You're running out of time. You need to take a math class next semester so you can fit in the stat classes your final two semesters."

I felt heat spread across my face. "I can't do math."

"Why not?"

"I-I've never done well in math. I'm not smart enough."

He pulled a three-ring binder from his bookcase and opened it, then ran his finger down a page until he found what he was looking for. "Math 35 meets graduation requirements."

"That's the math class for dummies, isn't it?"

"It's the math class for smart people who are math phobic. I know you're smart. If you've never done well in math, I suspect it's because you're math phobic." He leaned forward. "It's a small class, only about twenty students. I've heard good things about it from people who've taken it."

"I guess if I want to graduate, I have no choice."

At the beginning of the following semester, I arrived early for Math 35's first class and took a seat in the middle of the room where I could blend in and not be noticed. The girl sitting to my left leaned over. "Even if this is math for dummies, I can't do it. My name's Linda."

My shoulders slumped. "I can't do math either. I'm Cyndi."

A man in his early-thirties with gray-streaked brown hair that fell to his waist entered the room. Dressed in tattered jeans and a plaid flannel shirt so threadbare that both sleeves had worn through at the elbows, he set his books on the instructor's table and wrote "Math 35" on the board.

A number of us exchanged sideways glances. Underneath the course name he wrote "Phil." Turning to the class, he flicked his loose hair over his shoulder. "My name's plain ol' Phil. No Doctor or Mister in front of it. I'm just plain ol' Phil."

"Is he really an instructor?" I asked Linda, my new cohort in mathematical misery. "He doesn't look like one."

She rolled her eyes. "It's the dummy math class. Probably no one wants to teach it."

"Now let's get this straight," Plain ol' Phil continued. "No matter what you've heard, Math 35 is not the dummy math class."

Right, I thought, years of failure in math reinforcing my conviction that I wasn't intelligent enough to understand the simplest forms of mathematics. I glanced at my classmates and prayed I wouldn't be the dumbest one among them.

Plain ol' Phil's voice snapped me back to attention. "This class is for people who never had a teacher who knew *how* to teach math. I'm here to teach highly intelligent people — that's every one of you — who think they're math stupid. The class will be challenging. You'll have to work hard. Very hard. But if you show up for class and do all of the work, you'll know how to do math by the end of the semester and your final grade will reflect that. I've never had a student fail."

"Apparently he's never encountered anyone like me," Linda whispered.

"Or me." I opened my notebook.

Plain ol' Phil wrote the word "permutations" on the board next to a math formula that made as much sense to me as Egyptian hieroglyphs. "There goes my GPA," a voice behind me groaned.

A guy seated in the row ahead of me turned his head toward the back of the room. "That's it," he said, wide-eyed. "I'm done for." A number of students nodded their concurrence, me included.

My stomach twisted into a tight square knot. Five minutes into the first class of the semester and we were all done for.

Plain ol' Phil stopped writing, turned, and faced us. "I'd feel done for, too, if all a math teacher ever did was write formulas and numbers on the board and expect you to memorize them and come up with the right answer. But has anyone ever explained to you that math is found everywhere? It's all around us every single day from the simple to the complex. Mathematical measurements are used in cooking, medications, and in figuring out how much paint to buy for a room. Determining the affordability of monthly mortgage payments and the comparison of interest rates in fixed and variable rate loans over a determined period of time requires math. Knowing the miles-per-gallon of gasoline that our car uses, we can decide with certainty whether or not to fill the gas tank before driving through a desolate 150-mile stretch of road." He paused, his eyes scanning the classroom. "Let's get started."

Our class met three days a week, and every Friday we took a quiz on that week's lessons. To my astonishment, I earned an A on each one. The weekly tests weren't easy, but for the first time in our lives, my classmates and I were earning high grades in math.

The end of the semester arrived and Phil passed out the final exam, a comprehensive test covering all of the course's material. While the weekly quizzes accounted for 40% of the final grade, the final exam, worth 60%, would determine our grade for the course.

My mind filled with apprehension as the old thoughts returned that I was too dumb to do math. I looked at the exam's first question. My mind went blank as though I had never seen the material.

I skipped to the next question and the one after that with the same reaction. After a semester of excelling on weekly quizzes, my math phobia returned and I knew this final exam would incinerate my A. I framed my face with my hands and lowered my head, tears stinging my eyes, as I stared at the paper. It was true after all: I was dumb in math — and about to ruin my chance of graduating from college.

"You can do this," someone whispered in my ear. Startled, I turned toward the voice. Phil.

"I can't do it," my voice cracked. "I don't remember any of this."

Phil knelt at my side and pointed at the first question. "Remember how I taught this concept in class? I broke it down into small units and explained all of the parts. Then I explained how and why it's used. Remember?"

The steady gaze from his blue eyes threw a lifeline to me. My racing heart slowed. "Yes." My eyes locked on the only person who had made me think I might be able to do math. "I-I do remember."

"You can do this, Cyndi. You're smart. You passed every quiz. I know you understand everything on this exam. I know you can do this." Phil's words, sincere and honest, exuded confidence — confidence in *me*.

I took a deep breath, picked up my pencil, and tackled the first question. Rechecking my math, I knew I had the correct answer. I looked up to thank

Phil, but he had moved to another student. Just like he had done for me, Phil whispered encouraging words and I watched the young man's ashen face fill with healthy color. While I worked out math problems using formulas that had real meaning for me, Phil worked his way around the room.

A week later, I received my final grade—an A. My first A ever in math. The truth is, I earned that A. It was hard-fought and hard-won, but I didn't achieve the victory on my own. A man who believed it was as important to instill confidence in a student as it was to teach the subject matter had taught me to ignore past defeats and believe in my ability to succeed. Plain ol' Phil knew how to really teach and he touched hearts in ways that mattered far more than grades.

Day after day, I worked with my son during his third grade year, but in spite of my teaching skills and his desire to achieve, he struggled to learn.

"Will I ever get good grades, Mommy?"

"Yes. Yes, you will."

I could see in his eyes how badly he wanted to believe me. "You're smart, Justin — and I'm not saying that because I'm your mother. I mean it. You know that I'm a teacher and I know what I'm talking about. You are smart. You can do this. I know you can." I kissed his head, then leaned back and smiled. "Let's get to work."

Not so long ago I watched Justin graduate from his internal medicine residency program. A brilliant man strapped with a dyslexic learning challenge, Justin worked exceptionally hard to learn to read and achieve academic success. But during those times when he faltered, when he doubted his innate ability to succeed, I knew what to do. Plain ol' Phil's words came to life as I whispered them in my son's ear, "You're smart. You can do this. I know you can."

Cynthia Howerter

25

My Pampered Pooch

I've had many furry, four-legged friends but none more cherished than my golden retriever, Jonathan Douglass.

Johnny D, as I often called him, was a handsome guy with silky tan fur, floppy ears, and big brown eyes framed by dark eyelashes. He was good natured, people loving and an expert Frisbee catcher. With a few nudges of his head, he could coax anyone to scratch him behind his ears.

From his puppy to senior dog days, Jonathan never tired of making people laugh. When I took him for his daily walk, he often carried his big, white teddy bear in his mouth. He never wore a wristwatch but sat looking out the window in the afternoon so he could howl a few barks for Mark the mailman. I only had to say the word "car," and he stood soldier-straight by the kitchen door ready for a trip.

He was partial to table food and would spit out a piece of toast if offered without butter. Pizza, especially the crusts, liverwurst, and roasted chicken were some of his favorite foods. Once a week in the summer, he enjoyed a trip to Carvel for a kiddie-size vanilla ice cream cone. He was also a skilled eater of corn on the cob. When I twirled the cob, he licked the butter, then proceeded to munch on the corn down to the last kernel.

Jonathan loved to pose for pictures, especially at Christmas when he sat at the foot of Santa Paws. Decked out with a red Santa hat perched on his head, Jonathan stared at the camera but was really focused on the jar of opened peanut butter waving in the air. A few licks of the spoon was the reward for being a good boy.

When everyone wore Easter bonnets, Jonathan wore big, floppy, pink satin rabbit ears. Halloween was no exception. Wearing his costume, he was an expert trick-or-treater. Whether he was an aviator with a scarf around his neck and goggle covered eyes or Native American chief resplendent in a multi-colored feather headdress ready for a powwow, Jonathan rivaled any neighborhood youngster. He was a charmer wearing his pink ballerina tutu, but he couldn't quite manage the toe shoes.

As a senior, Jonathan loved his Wicked Witch of the West costume. Resplendent in black pointed hat and flowing cape decorated with an orange spider, he posed with a stoic look on his face. He didn't appear ready to scare ghosts and goblins nor could he ride away on a broom.

Johnny loved to trick or treat. Together, we made the rounds to the local deli where he gobbled his treat of a few slices of cheese and then to the bank where the teller handed out giant size Milk Bone biscuits. After the final stops to see relatives, it was time to head home. Jonathan was done trick or treating for another year. After his supper, he lazily trudged to his favorite spot in my bedroom and plopped down on the rug. After a few big yawns, Johnny went to sleep.

Jonathan was eleven years old when he trick or treated as the Wicked Witch of the West. In May of the following year when he had his twelfth birthday, he could no longer run, jump or catch a Frisbee in the air. His steps were slower, his hearing level reduced, but his nose still sniffed out his favorite treats. Johnny developed slight cataracts, but glasses were not an option.

As the end of summer approached, it became more challenging for Jonathan to walk. On the morning of August 30, Jonathan woke up, had trouble standing and struggled to walk. The few steps he managed were done with a severe limp. But, he didn't lose his hearty appetite. He gobbled what became his final dinner of roasted salmon and the only dog food he liked, Kibbles and Bits. With a heavy heart, I called his vet. Tears streamed down my cheeks. I did not want to make the hard decision I knew I faced.

As a senior, Jonathan had difficulty hopping into the car so his vet made a house call when needed. That Friday, his doctor made a visit and diagnosed a possible torn ligament. "I can give him an injection, but it's temporary," said his vet. It would only prolong Jonathan's discomfort. But my Jonathan couldn't walk. I made the gut-wrenching decision to put my wonderful, lovable golden to sleep.

At 6:30 P.M. in our living room I held Jonathan in my arms and told him how much I loved him and would miss him. As I held him close and stroked his head, I repeated words he loved to hear. "Jonathan you are such a good boy; you are such a good boy."

As I pressed my tear stained face to his furry one, he quietly closed his eyes. Peacefully he crossed the Rainbow Bridge and went to doggy heaven. A picture of Jonathan in his Wicked Witch of the West Halloween costume adorns the front of the cherry wood box that holds his cremated remains.

Jonathan Douglass was a funny, lovable one-hundred pound goofy golden and cherished member of our family. Johnny was a gentleman always ready to lift a paw and shake hands. I miss him and always will. He gave us, and we gave him, over twelve years of love and memories to cherish for a lifetime.

My Johnny D was a wonderful, loyal friend who brought a smile to everyone he met. A pet-parent couldn't ask for anyone better.

Beverly Sce

26

A Two-sided Love Story

To go from Point A to Point B for an eighty-seven-year-old mom is not always as short a trip as it might seem it should be. This is a romance story of two kinds, my early love life and the love life I have lived, so hang on and take the ride down memory lane with me.

I was born in Deep Creek, a village in Norfolk County, Portsmouth, Virginia, child number eight to a mom who had not wanted any more children. I did not know the story of my birth until the night before my husband and I left for New York, enroute to Pakistan, to serve as missionaries.

It seems she and God had a little time together one morning and she told him if he would help her love this baby she would give it back to him for whatever he wanted of it. With tears in her eyes, she told me the story, then said, "But I never knew God would take you so far away from me." It would be five years before she saw me again, along with our three little ones.

Like others in those post depression years, my parents struggled to care for their children. The one advantage was the plot of land they were able to buy and have a small farm life. I was strong willed, maybe a daredevil or a tomboy who had more fun than sissy girls like my sister, and I loved the outdoors. But I don't think they believed I would live to adulthood. Bronchial troubles plagued me. When I got a cough, I had to stay home, and I would beg to go outside. My Mom would let me stand in a protected corner, next to the chimney where it was warm, just for a few minutes. I loved it.

In high school, I was on the student council and a cheerleader, involved in lots of activities, especially in my church. When I was sixteen, a handsome 6'2" blond came to our church, and we got acquainted. He was in boarding school in another state, so I did not see him after school started, but when he returned home at Christmas and during the summer, we dated. I really thought he was "the one." We had similar goals and I was falling for him, hook line and sinker. I thought he would be my husband some day.

We went away to the same Christian college. These were the post war days, 1945-46. Many service people were returning and could go to college under the GI bill. In order to accommodate everyone, the college had three shifts for meals and classes. He was on first shift; I was on third. College rules about dating were strict. That meant we did not get to be together. One day I saw him walking across campus with another girl. A short time later there was a formal program when he could have invited me, but did not. I said, "That's it!" Then I met Richard.

When it was my turn to invite a boy for my literary society's all-day outing. I invited him. We were in a group, so I did not get to know much about him. In turn, he invited me to go to church with him. He was quiet; I am outgoing, talkative, and I began to ask questions.

"Were you in service?"

"Yes."

"Oh, how long?"

"Three years."

"Were you overseas?"

"Yes."

"How long?"

"A year and a half."

That was just about the extent of the conversation. After I got to know him, I asked why he did not talk more on that first date. He said, "You are not supposed to talk in church." I told him I was about to throw him over.

Our next date was a soccer game, almost another disaster. It was nine-week exam time, but, some of us gals may have been more interested in a MRS. degree than a BA — you know how it goes. When he kept talking about how much studying he had to do, I got disgusted. I said, "Do you want to go study?"

About five minutes later he said, "No."

So much time had passed, I had forgotten what I said, so I asked again. He thought I had asked, "Do you want to go steady?"

It seems his grandmother who had moved to Florida from the mid-west had had a little talk with him after he got out of the service. When she knew he was going to college in the south, she told him, "You have to watch those Southern girls; they are fast!"

I worked in the library. One day we decided to meet in there to study. That's where I got to know more about him. There was a large world map on the wall. He told me he was born in India, showed me where, and told me he wanted to go to the northwest corner, on the border of Afghanistan, the frontier.

I had no idea where it was, but I knew I was headed for China. We continued to date for a while. He had been around the world. I was from Deep Creek and had hardly been to the city of Portsmouth! Well, not quite, but I really knew little about the wide world. It was just the beginning of why this romance could not be right.

While still in the library, he showed me what I call his pedigree, something of which I hardly knew the meaning. We went into the files where he wanted to look for the book, *Who's Who in America*. I was not even aware there was such a book. His grandfather was written up in it as author, statesman, archaeologist, educator — the whole bit.

Richard was from a highly educated family. How in the world would he fit into the lifestyle I had lived in the country? It was a little like the rich-man poor-girl thing. I would find later the whole family were all highly educated, but dedicated Christians who had lived lives of service. I was not from an educated family. I was the first one to go to college. A sister and a brother had been offered scholarships, but there was no money, so they missed out.

We continued to date and despite the differences, we were falling in love. Friends were encouraging each of us, saying we belonged together. He was headed for India. I was planning on China, to work in an orphanage. Neither of us was willing to give in. We broke up.

It was hard. I dated another boy; he dated another girl. That went on for a few months. It was in 1947 when the news came that India was dividing into two countries. The Muslims, people God had laid on his heart, would be in Pakistan and the Hindus would have India. About the same time, China closed the doors to missionaries. Those two events put us back together. We settled the matter. We would go to the northwest frontier of the new country of Pakistan.

We like to say God had to make a whole new country just to get us back together!

That Christmas, I got my ring. We finished our BA degrees, and got married, lived in an eighteen-foot trailer for the next year while he worked on his MA degree. In May, we were invited to go with a group from college to attend a TEAM Missionary Conference in Chicago. It is what is called an interdenominational faith mission. That meant we had to raise our own money for support, travel and outfit. They were planning to send several couples to Pakistan. We liked what we learned and wanted to be among the first to go. I worked part time in a department store and did the typing for his work on the MA degree. He was a great student and completed it in one year plus summer school. While he was doing that in the summer, I worked in three different children's summer camps. One morning, I woke up nauseated. The older ladies in camp had to tell me I was expecting. Richard's first words were, "I want my child to be born overseas like I was."

We got word we had been accepted by the mission, and on Dec. 23, 1950, boarded the ship in New York, bound for Pakistan. I think we broke all mission records in the length of time it took for us to raise our money and leave. God was supplying, and He can do that!

"It's just beautiful," I said, looking around at my new surroundings that frosty January morning. The scene was a small cantonment area in a bowl-like setting with a ring of snow-clad Himalayan Mountain foothills, set 3,500 feet up in the northwest frontier corner of Pakistan. It was here I began my journey into the deeper world of faith. I have never lost my love for that land.

The air was crisp and patches of snow were still scattered around, a welcome change after riding through the dust of the Sindh Desert, 1,000 miles away. It had been thirty-six hours since we boarded the train in Karachi and said goodbye to my father-in-law who left his mission work in India to meet us. He had crossed the border to welcome back his son and we were privileged to spend the night in the same Methodist mission house where Richard had spent part of his childhood.

They reminisced about the past, laughed and sometimes spoke the strange tongue of Urdu while reliving old times. For me, everything was new. With this new venture, we had become career missionaries with TEAM, expecting to spend our lives in this northwest corner of the new country of Pakistan, just as Richard's parents had in India, but this was tribal area with a language written in characters I would have to learn. I was still a talker, so I did learn it. It became a wonderful link to knowing the people.

I knew we were there by God's leading. Our baby, still in my *bacche dana* (Urdu for "baby carrier"), was born a month later, in the Mission Hospital in Taxila, fifty-five miles away.

Archaeological and historical records let us know Taxila was a village created by Alexander the Great's army over 2,300 years earlier. The United Presbyterians had founded the Christian hospital many years before.

I have never doubted that choosing to be God's servant in foreign lands was anything but a great experience, even though not every day was "the best day of my life." There was the adjustment to new foods, new language, and a whole new world which I had to learn to navigate through.

I am the better for all of that.

God gave us five wonderful children and blessed me and Richard with sixty-four years together.

It's as if our every step in life was planned and maneuvered. I am sure it was God who did just that.

Myrtle Thompson

27

All Those Years Ago

I'm talking all about how to give.

George Harrison

As my birthday neared, I wondered what my son would choose this time. What events would he recreate? Which of my life's milestones would he bring into sharp focus through the medium of music? Heaven knows, and Steve too, how much I need some cheering.

In 1964, when *I Want to Hold Your Hand* hit American pop charts, Steve was only six, but he listened raptly when I chattered about my high school journalism students dancing the Frug and the Watusi on the Lloyd Thaxton Show, airing from nearby Los Angeles.

Since his dad worked nights, Steve and I had evenings to ourselves. While I corrected homework papers, we listened to legendary sportscaster Vin Scully call the play-by-play on the radio for our beloved Dodgers. Or we strolled to the library to stock up on his favorite Dr. Seuss and Maurice Sendak storybooks.

Now we began to follow rock and roll. We tuned in the dance shows of the day, *Shindig*, *Hullabaloo*, Dick Clark's *American Bandstand*. Steve spent his allowance joining Beatles fan clubs. I heard empathy in his voice as he read to me from the newsletters about children in Kenya and the Philippines that the clubs sponsored for tuition and books.

Sometimes we brought our BLTs and lemonade into the living room, dining while we caught up on the latest scoop. "Listen to what George Harrison's sister says," Steve would exclaim, excited at having a personal connection with one of the Fab Four.

In the meantime, my students transitioned from the Beach Boys, and Jan and Dean, to the British Invasion. "Which side would you take?" I asked Steve, discussing debates on the merits of The Dave Clark Five versus Herman's Hermits. Steve remained loyal to the mop top Beatles, his "fave raves." We lamented not securing tickets to the Hollywood Bowl appearances, and in l966 envied our neighbor who took her sons to the concert at Dodger Stadium.

By 1968, Steve hunkered down at the kitchen counter every Wednesday night as KHJ's Sam Riddle counted down the *Boss 30*. He meticulously recorded the hits one by one in his blue notebook. He already had been collecting singles for well over a year. In the meantime, I had changed jobs, so now raced down the 405 toward the Cudahy Department of Public Social Services office, also tuned to KHJ, grooving on the Beatles, the Box Tops, Linda Ronstadt, and even all 7 minutes and 11 seconds of Richard Harris' *MacArthur Park*.

"I hear music in my head," Steve once confided. I asked if he wanted to take piano or guitar lessons. "No," he confessed. "I just love to listen." Over the years his collection stockpiled. He turned from singles to LPs, and then to 8-tracks, cassettes, and finally to CDs. In recent decades he has shared some obscure cuts with Southland Golden Oldies radio stations.

When I joined the Peace Corps in l987, Steve provided me with the first of his special gifts. He transferred to cassette all of the Beatles numbers from his albums. On balmy Saturday mornings in Belize City, I hand-laundered my towels and sheets, listening to *Your Mother Should Know* and *Magical Mystery Tour*.

Three years ago on my birthday, the first time capsule arrived. Steve went through his collection and made me a recording of the top songs from fall l967 to spring l968, my first year with DPSS. Then retired in the country, I played the recording every time I made the seventy-mile drive to Spokane. As I listened to The Cowsills, Lulu, and other chart toppers of that era, I felt the years rolling back. I became 30 years old once again, driving around Los Angeles, waiting for my future to unfold with each song, each mile, each day.

At Christmas, another recording arrived. This time Steve chose my 21st birthday, just months after he had been born. Until I played my gift, I had forgotten carrying infant Steve around the house, boogying to Bobby Darin's *Splish Splash*, and two-stepping to Laurie London's *He's Got the Whole World in His Hands*.

Shortly thereafter, my son's dad died. When Steve visited me, I dragged out a duffle bag of old photos to show him pictures of his father and me in l955, the year we got engaged and married. "You looked so happy," he said.

We had been.

When I opened my package on my 70th birthday, memories of 1955 flooded back. Steve had labeled the recording, "Terri's 18th Birthday — Plus," and had included "a nice mix of the old music fighting for time with the new rock 'n roll," with highlights from that summer and fall.

And sure enough, there it all was, the songs that his dad and I courted to, Roger Williams' romantic ballad, *Autumn Leaves*, following Chuck Berry's *Maybelline*. As if it were only yesterday, I remember getting seasick on the Catalina ferry as we sailed back from our Avalon honeymoon; decorating our first apartment with the wedding gifts; snagging my first full-time job at Pacific Tel and Tel.

My second husband died this past spring. Steve's collection does not extend up to the late '90's when Ken and I first met. Nonetheless, my son has promised some treats. "I'm going to take you through four decades this time, Mom," he wrote in an email. And when my birthday came, just weeks after my husband's death, I found solace in listening to the tunes of happier days. Here were the June 28's of 1957, 1961, 1971, 1975, and 1981, plus a note that promises even more happy moments to come.

At first I sighed as I heard *All Those Years Ago*, George Harrison's tribute to John Lennon, killed just six months earlier, but soon my heart lifted as the Oak Ridge Boys rocked *Elvira*. I suddenly recalled how songs that year eased me through a difficult transition.

The recollections of Marcel Proust's hero in *Remembrance of Things Past* were triggered by the taste of a Madeline cookie.

Some people claim to remember best through scents. For me, nothing tugs the elusive shadows of my past into the shimmering sunlight of this current moment like the songs on my time capsules.

Steve's recordings are candid snapshots of loving moments in my life, framed in melody.

Terri Elders

28

Love for a Grandchild

When my son told me I was going to be a grandmother I was thrilled beyond words, but the nearer the delivery date, the more conflicted I became. What if I didn't love my grandchild enough? I have no idea where such an absurd question came from. If we give all the love we are able to give, it is always enough.

Perhaps because I had loved my son, an only child, so fiercely as he was growing up, it was impossible for me to imagine that I could love another child in the same way.

In fact, the law of divine multiplication is perhaps best reflected in love. The more love we give, the more love we have to give. The more we give away, the more we get back. The more we are loved, the more we want to love.

My fears were put to rest the moment I held Alexander Talmadge in my arms. He had a head of blond hair so thick it looked as if he was wearing a wig. His long fingers wrapped around mine by reflex, but it felt as if he was accepting me as an important person in his life. When he opened his big blue eyes and stared at me, it felt like we were linked by eternity. Past, present, and future were all bound up in that moment of life regenerated.

I live several hours away from my son and I feared that my little bundle of joy would not remember me from one visit to the next. Whether he remembered or not as a helpless infant, he was always happy to see me, and indulged my hugs and kisses with patience. He rewarded me with his smiles and snuggles.

As he began to communicate, I was ecstatic when he uttered his first, "Gran." Of course I heard it long before anyone else recognized it, but I was certain he knew me. We had far more than a DNA connection.

His toddler years were a flurry of activity. He always had a new toy to share, a game to play, or something he wanted to show me when I went to visit. I was so proud of every single new accomplishment as his intelligence grew and his communication skills increased.

He grew quickly to be a child of deep thought and reflection. His questions were endless.

I was especially interested in his perception of God since his dad had developed a keen awareness at an early age. One night he took my face in his hands and stared hard into my eyes as he asked, "Gran, are you an angel?"

Where he got such a notion is beyond me.

A few weeks down the road he wanted to know if God was my friend. I assured him that God was my best friend and would be his friend also.

In the meantime, I was delighted to hear that another grandchild was on the way. Once again I began to fret about my capacity to love another child as much as I love Alex. It seemed humanly impossible for me to duplicate the same amount of love for any other living creature.

I carried that concern with me all the way to the delivery date when we were invited into the room to greet our little princess for the first time. When she was placed in my arms, the sound of my heart stretching was almost audible. I had never held a baby girl of my own, and couldn't imagine how one little granddaughter could open up the world in a whole new way.

She and her brother are as different as male and female. Alex's broad shoulders and Maren's willowy shape were only one of the many differences.

She has learned at a different rate, taken interest in different things, and mastered certain skills successfully all on her own timetable. She loves to talk and sing whether anyone is listening or not. Alex tends to be more quiet and reflective. Her favorite pastime is following her brother and doing things to demand his attention.

I love everything about her, from her tendency to want to straighten things and put them away to her big blue eyes and mischievous grin. She is truly a learning experience for me on every level.

At four-years-old Alex has begun to wonder about prayer and talking to God. On my visits, I pray for each child, and encourage them to talk to God. At two, Maren is happy with memorized prayers, but Alex is already trying to find his way to his Heavenly Father.

"Gran, when I talk to God, why doesn't he ever talk back? If he hears me, why doesn't he say something to me?"

"He hears every prayer you pray, and he does speak to you."

"How come I can't hear him?" he wanted to know.

"You have to listen with your heart," I tried to explain. "You will know it's God talking to you because he always says things like, 'I love you, Alex. You are a good boy, Alex. Don't be afraid, Alex, because I will take care of you.'"

"God doesn't say bad things, does he?" Alex wanted to know.

"No, he doesn't," I assured him. "If you hear something bad it will only be your imagination. God will only say good things."

He lay there under the covers silently for a while thinking. "Poop. That probably wasn't God, was it? God doesn't talk about things like that. He probably doesn't know about things like that." He was as sincere as a four-year-old could possibly be.

I laughed to myself. "Good example," I said. "That was your imagination and not God talking to you."

I never know what either of these two precious babies is going to say to me, show me, or want me to do with them. I cherish every moment we spend together.

I have never felt more love in my life than when the two of them attack me at the door when I arrive, showering me with hugs and kisses. They aren't old enough to pretend, as many adults in our lives will do. What they give of themselves from their hearts is pure. They aren't trying to manipulate anyone. They are not in a contest for attention.

They simply love.

Judith Victoria Hensley

29

Deer Stand Christmas

I'm going out to warm up the truck," Dad whispered as loud as he could without waking Mom.

Mom would stay at the house during our dad-and-daughter hunting trips and keep the fireplace blazing while she baked her amazing homemade biscuits. Mom's biscuits with jelly she canned from blackberries out of their own garden, dad's unmatched barbeque brisket, and more always awaited us for lunch when we returned from hunting. Christmas break from college just couldn't get any better than this."

"Ok, I'm almost ready," I whispered back.

It was early in the morning, still dark, and I could not wait. I looked forward to this all year.

I borrowed Mom's Carhartt coveralls and layered to keep warm. Dad and I finished putting our coffee in a thermos, and I grabbed the rest of our supplies before heading out to the truck. I was quiet on the drive, basking in the moment, thinking about how much I enjoyed these times. Dad always said his hunting was especially good when I was with him, that someway my being there made a difference. Though the compliment was appreciated, I doubted I brought him any better odds. Yet, hearing the encouraging words showed me, as I got older, a growing and much needed friendship with my parents.

School had been especially difficult for me as a child and remained so throughout college. I wondered at times if I would graduate high school let alone finish college. To make matters worse, I was among the easiest of children to tease in grade school as at times the simplest concepts took longer for me to grasp than most students my age. Severe health problems made learning and many other activities extra challenging.

Still, Christmases with my parents kept me going while I was making every effort to complete my education. Though we shared other meaningful times during each year, my parents always did their best to make Christmas breaks special. Mom and Dad were among the few who understood how difficult, most days, even small tasks could be for me. Those times with them would mean more to me in the years after college than I could imagine."

"Ok, we're here," Dad said.

We pulled up as close as we could to one of our favorite hunting spots. I tried to force my eyes to wake up enough so I could ease out of the truck and make my way over with a flashlight.

Dad scattered corn while I carefully climbed up to scrunch into the small deer stand. Once we settled in, Dad shelled some pecans for us to munch as we sipped hot coffee and began our wait.

Sometimes those old stands would get cold, but we didn't let the chill bother us. To me, all that really mattered was the sweet time I shared with my dad as we sat quietly watching for deer, whispering about whatever was on our minds. We would talk about Mom, the house, past Christmases, dreams, memories, stuff we found funny, anything. At times it was all we could do to keep from laughing out loud so as to not scare off the deer. Sometimes, when we went hunting in the evening, I brought a small, battery operated color television and we watched football with the sound off while looking out for deer. We grinned big and mouthed, "Touchdown!" and cheered silently when our team scored.

"Your mother is smelling up the house right now with her biscuits," Dad whispered as he handed me a freshly shelled pecan.

"She is. I can taste them already. I smiled. "Thanks for bringing me out here, Dad. This is so much fun. This place is calming, peaceful."

"I'm glad you like coming with me," he said.

We chatted, pausing to slowly lean in and look through narrow openings in expectation of deer wandering into view. Spotting birds or an occasional rabbit was also fun.

In the stillness, I would talk to God about things that weighed heavy on my heart. Sitting in a deer stand with my dad was a place I could clear my head, consider the past year, and pray about goals I wanted to reach in the next. Most of all I prayed about my desperate need for physical healing from chronic pain that took many years for doctors to effectively treat.

It seemed like nothing short of a miracle that I finished college and graduate school. I spent much of my college years and afterwards hoping God had a plan for my life and that He would somehow let me survive. My health became so poor at one point that I began to close out each day by thanking God for another day, and asking Him to take care of my parents in case I did not make it through the night. There came a point where the doctors could do little to help me, or what they did offer only made things worse. All I knew to do was pray, depend on God completely, and know that my life was in His hands. I began to accept that if He wanted me to live another day, then I would live another day. That acceptance became my only strength for a long time. I learned that if God had a plan for my life, He would make everything work out in His time. He would make a way in my impossible situation.

It was during those hunting trips I realized how particularly encouraging the way Dad discussed things with me was. He would talk to me as if I was smart, and listen as though I had good ideas worth hearing on any subject. He understood that many times I didn't feel well or intelligent, even though I was in college. He knew that I felt way behind my peers because of overwhelming challenges. Dad often humored me to get through problems, while reminding me that God had special plans for me, and telling me not to worry. He had a way of making Mom and me laugh while acting like nothing was funny, only to make us laugh all the harder.

The best part, though, is how they both taught me to laugh at myself, how to find humor in the midst of frustrations. While they had it tough growing up, married young and started out with nothing, they showed me how to value the most important things in life, how to persevere, and that with God, all things are possible.

Christmas had become a gift of memories about my loving family. I learned that someday I want to marry a man who will be a friend like my dad has been to me and to my mom through their fifty years together. And I realized there was always something more waiting for me on those hunting trips with my dad, a unique Christmas gift designed just for me in that special place and season of the year. It wasn't something that could be placed under a Christmas tree.

Within the reality of winter's cold, and silence of the woods, God convinced me He knows me well, knows exactly what He is doing and has a grip on my life that nothing can break. Though challenges were difficult to manage, God's love restored me again and again at Christmastime in an unlikely place.

God gave me the family I needed to help me along during the toughest years. I am reminded today of God's redeeming love, and that in the least likely places He does something big. His greatest gift arrived long ago, as a babe in a Bethlehem manger. He showed up for me in a rickety old deer stand. Packaged in a way I could cherish for a lifetime, He brought me the best and most important gifts of all — those loving moments.

Amanda Hughes

30

Surprised by Love

I grew up in a loving home. I always knew my parents and extended family loved me, no matter what. But there were some special times I don't think I'll ever forget.

It was 1999 and I turned thirty that year. I lived in Southern California, about forty miles east of Los Angeles. My family was scattered all over the state, except for my parents, who lived in South Carolina. My brother Jim, and his wife Shawna, were the nearest family I had, about sixty miles away. We didn't see each other often since they were so busy with their family.

One day in early July, Jim called and asked what I was doing for my birthday in a few weeks. When I told him I had no plans, he asked if I'd like to come up that weekend and we'd celebrate it together. I was delighted he'd offered and immediately took him up on it. There would be Jim, Shawnna, their daughter Brittany, son Josh, and me.

I looked forward to it and told all my friends in the Sunday school class how excited I was and that it meant a lot that Jim would think to do that. They were excited for me.

Over the next couple weeks Jim called to make sure things were still on for the date. I said yes and told him how eager I was to see them again.

On a crisp, clear day I drove along the freeway to Jim's and marveled at the mountains before me. I thought of how much it meant to see them again. I looked forward to the afternoon and evening ahead.

When I got to their home, Jim welcomed me and said, "Let's go out on the back porch and enjoy the views." I followed him and when I stepped outside, twenty people greeted me yelling, "Surprise!"

I stepped back, wide-eyed, and blown away to see all my family there. My grandma, my aunts and uncles from central California were there, and my parents had come all the way from South Carolina.

I shook my head in disbelief.

As if that weren't enough shock, I saw several friends from my Sunday school class. How in the world did Jim know how to contact them?

Then I discovered I wasn't dressed for the occasion. This was a luau.

"Didn't you get the note?" Mom teased.

Jim failed to mention that one, of course, when he invited me for the day. But Mom had brought a full-length red Hawaiian dress for me so I'd fit in. Too funny.

I later learned that Jim and Shawnna had been orchestrating the whole thing for about a month. They contacted family members and had them park on another block so I wouldn't suspect anything when I drove up.

As for my friends from church? Jim had asked Mom if she had any contact information for them. She had one person's e-mail address so she passed it along. Jim e-mailed my friend and told her of the surprise party he had planned. She, in turn, e-mailed the Sunday school class so people would come and join the fun. Shawnna had the whole house and backyard decked out with Hawaiian décor and lots of food and drinks.

The fact that Jim and Shawnna would go to all that trouble for me was huge. I realized that even though we rarely see each other, they love me. It was a wonderful time and is a special memory I carry with me, even so many years later.

Ellen Andersen

31

A "Step" of Faith

The summer had taken on a new routine. After work I would head down the highway to see my Dad, in the hospital doing his best to beat the evilness known as cancer. My Mom was always there, and the room was usually crowded with more family and visitors. This day in August was different.

After hugs and kisses all around, my sister motioned for me to go out into the hallway. My sister is a Nurse Practitioner at the same hospital and was one of our family's biggest blessings throughout those awful months. She gave me the Doctor's latest news, putting an actual amount of time left on my father's life expectancy. Three to six months.

I felt the blood rush down through my whole body. My heart started to beat faster and my eyes blurred with tears. While we knew things were not good, I did not expect to hear those words. Three to six months.

Now what? How do you start to truly process those words? When I went home that night I wrote a letter to my dad. I needed to write out my feelings. I just typed quickly from my heart. I did not care about proper grammar or punctuation. You see, this man was my stepdad. My father was killed when I was five-years-old, and this man was a gift. I wanted him to know how I felt about him.

This is what I needed my father to know before he left this world.

> Dad. *The English Dictionary*'s definition of a stepfather is, "a man who has married one's mother after the death or divorce of one's father."
>
> Although this is true, it barely describes what you have meant to me since you *stepped* into my life all those years ago. I had no idea how much you would mean to me and to my family when we first met at Camp of the Woods. You were Uncle Jack in the striped tiger velour shirt who became my father figure when I was eight-years-old.

"Mom, you married a winner," was something I would say with some sarcasm when I was young, but even though I pushed you away back then, you won my heart over and over again throughout my lifetime.

You taught me and those around me so much, Dad. You always put others before yourself. You believed in hard work, and built a family business that I am proud to be a part of. You loved my mom with great respect and patience.

You have taught my boys what a perfect gentleman looks like. You are the best Pop my kids could ever ask for, having a perfect balance of play, guidance and love. All my kids loved to sit by your side and read with you. They also loved to play ball with you, and know you were sitting on the sidelines through countless games and always cheered with pride.

Your love of history has rubbed off on at least one of your grandchildren. I relied on you often to explain your views on current events and politics because I had little time or interest to become an expert on some of those things.

You have always been my biggest fan and source of encouragement, whether it was my cooking or the kind of mom I have tried to be. You always made me feel like your own daughter, nothing "step" about it. I would have been lost however, without you "stepping" in whenever I needed you. You always made sure things in my life were being taken care of...changing my screens to storms, taking my truck for oil changes, making sure I had cash in my wallet for rides home from the lake, etc. I always knew you were there for me.

I had the honor and pleasure of working with you for several years. You were an excellent salesman and business owner. When I came in for work you would say something that made me smile, like, "Ahh, the indoor air quality just improved around here," or "Morning honey, don't you look nice today." We were a good pricing team. You priced, I typed. You proofed, I corrected. You re-proofed and I printed. We were a well-run machine. I loved how much you enjoyed bragging about your grandchildren to customers. Your face would just light up when you talked about them.

I have so many special memories of being up at Brant Lake, or North Woods, as you call it. Thank you for all that you did up there to give our family such a wonderful place to stay close, relax, and enjoy the quiet beauty of that place. Some of my favorite memories are: staining the deck with you, your taking the little ones for tractor rides, all the boat rides...every one of my kids got to drive the boat with Pop. Also, the amount of love and respect that your little church family had for you and Mom, seeing you come out in those Daisy Duke cut off shorts (actually that is one memory I wish I *could* get rid of), and of course all the trips to Crossroads for ice cream. That place was very special to you. Thank you again for it.

Your faith has always influenced me. You passed on a strong legacy of dependency on, and gratitude to your Heavenly Father. You loved to sing and had a beautiful strong voice that you used to praise your Savior. You loved to pray. You prayed without ceasing. Sometimes that *without ceasing* part would cause a nudge under the table because Mom's pot roast was getting cold. But you taught us the importance of bringing every need to, and thanking God for every blessing.

You said often, "No one loves you like your mother." I can understand that on several levels. I just don't want you to leave this earth not understanding the place you hold in our hearts and the powerful love that is felt by your wife, your children, your grandchildren, your brothers and sisters, your aunts, uncles, nieces, nephews, cousins and friends. Your heart must be filled with so many precious memories as faces come to your mind. I pray that those memories will stay with you now as you rest, and make you smile.

You have been through so much in the past several years, and my heart has hurt for you. You have taken this with grace and dignity and gentleness because that is who you are. We will continue to pray for a miracle, but when you have had enough, I will understand. My heart will break and I will miss you terribly, but I will see you at another time in another place.

Thank you for being in my life, Dad. I don't believe that you just *stepped* in. I believe that you were placed into my life by a loving God who knew exactly the type of father that an eight-year-old girl needed all those years ago.

I love you, Dad.

I wanted to say these things *to* him, while he was alive; not *about* him after he was gone.

I waited a few weeks before I sat on the side of his bed and read the letter to him. It was a beautiful, heart-breaking time. As I held his hand, he smiled and shook his head and told me he did not deserve the words that I spoke. He folded the letter and put into a drawer. No one except us and my mom knew about the letter.

We did not get our three months. God claimed him on October 26. Mom asked if I would read the letter at his Memorial Service. I agreed and my oldest son came up and stood with me in case I could not get through it.

The letter touched many hearts that day. Copies were made for relatives who asked. As hard as it was, I loved sharing my feelings and letting everyone know what a great man my dad was; but most of all, I was so grateful that my father was able to know just what an incredible "Step" of faith and love he was to me.

Shari Struyk

32

The Awesome Insignificance of Love

Sometimes my mental epiphanies arrive like a dousing of cold water. One such mind-boggling realization came in an unexpected way — petting my precious little six-pound rescue cat.

Let me backpedal. I like dogs. Not cats. To me, cats are aloof and haughty. Cats don't follow their human with unabashed adoration. Cats just sleep, eat, and scratch furniture. Cats never come when you call them. Plain and simple…I don't like cats.

That is, I didn't until a certain scrawny stray black cat appeared one day and insisted on following my dog and me on our daily walks. Not only did this meowing little creature shadow us as we made our mile trek twice a day, she made repeated attempts to leap into my arms, or, when I sat on the porch, to crawl onto my lap and snuggle. I countered this brazen attack with repeated attempts of my own, waving arms and legs like a ninny, hoping to shoo her away. A veritable tug-of-war.

I lost.

Needless to say, after three weeks of this emotional nagging, I adopted a stray black cat with beautiful green eyes. Or, rather, a stray black cat with beautiful green eyes adopted me. Whatever. I now have a rescue dog *and* a rescue kitty — the latter lavishing more unadulterated love on me than I'd ever experienced before. Talk about kitty kisses! My little black mini-panther leaps into my arms every time I return from an extended visit and literally covers my face with licks from her sandpaper tongue.

The epiphany? If a "dumb" creature — an insignificant stray cat, of which the world seems to have too many — can love that simply and purely and whole-heartedly, how much more can a human being love?

Human beings, made in the image and likeness of God, should be able to change the course of mighty rivers with their love. If a tiny-scrap-of-a-kitten is capable of so much tenderness and adulation, how much more sensitivity and admiration can a human being produce?

My little cat has taught me more about the power and awesomeness of love than anything I've read or seen in all my years on this earth. Verses like "Now these three remain: faith, hope and love. But the greatest of these is love" (1 Corinthians 13:13 NIV) seem crystal-clear now. Love is overwhelming, remarkable, breathtaking, incredible, extraordinary. Love is one big, powerful WOW.

We all need to start loving like little stray kittens. Wouldn't *that* knock the world off its axis!

Theresa Jenner Garrido

33

God, the Cosmos, and Me

I know God loves me, and always has, considering my spiritual timeline started in a dead-state, and brought me to near-zealous, and pretty much keeps me in a constant state of Spirit-Awareness.

Don't get me wrong when I use that term. I'm not into the New Age movement or any sort of cult. It's just the term I use to feel the Holy Spirit that Jesus gave to us after His ascension.

But I'm not perfect. I have my highs and lows. When I pray, I always pray to God, and expect the Holy Spirit to listen and help out with any requests or guidance I may need. Romans 8:26 NLT says the Holy Spirit helps us in our distress. For we don't even know what we should pray for, nor how we should pray. But the Holy Spirit prays for us with groanings that cannot be expressed in words. Therefore, I fully expect the Holy Spirit to give me the right answer I need if I have a question.

When I'm drifting toward sin or a gray-area, the Holy Spirit advises me the course of action to take or avoid, or even recommend to others when necessary. The Lord says, "No John!" and I back off. It's my prayer that my thoughts and the thoughts of the Holy Spirit are merged.

The greatest way Jesus showed His love for us is his being crucified on the cross. He felt the pain of sin (which he didn't commit) so that I could be forgiven by believing in Him and accepted Him into my heart and life.

His forgiveness for me is why I need to forgive others. Matthew 18:21-22 NLT tells us, "Peter came to him and asked, 'Lord, how often should I forgive someone who sins against me? Seven times?' 'No!' Jesus replied, 'seventy times seven!'"

Seventy times seven is symbolic of how many times we should forgive others. The number of sins we need forgiveness for, myself in particular, over a lifetime is much more.

Christ on the Cross, the Holy Spirit, and God's grace are not the only ways that God has shown me He loves me, although any one of them is more than sufficient. When I was lost, God took the time to show me through science and nature how infinite He is.

I noticed the physical laws of the universe, like gravity, energy, stars, planets and the galaxies and realized that God is a creator of the things that baffle some human scientists.

God's creation is not only one of order, but also of beauty.

I can look at the wonders of nature and praise God's creation at face value, never mind the cosmos. He created all this nature for us to just believe in Him, for who He is. For He is, He was, and is yet to come!

So I try to stop, whether I'm in the city or in a rural area and say, "Thank You, O Lord, for this mysterious and wondrous Earth."

I thank Him that we can receive the Holy Spirit and know that God loves us all... all the time.

John Chaney

34

Distance Makes No Difference

"If you girls break up that bread into bite sized pieces, I'll show you how we make bread pudding."

Oh, surely Sister Monique was kidding! My sister Marie and I eyed the mountain of bread stacked on the table before us then looked at each other in disbelief. There had to be fifty loaves of bread on the table. But who could refuse the cheerful little nun? We sure couldn't. Sister Monique's sparkling Spanish eyes and sweet smile framed by her stiff white bonnet drew us in with the first glance she cast in our direction.

She was not to be taken lightly even though her frame seemed lost in the folds her billowing religious habit. Sister Monique ran the kitchen of St. Michael's Home for the Aged in Philadelphia with a no-nonsense style softened by her cheerful and fun loving heart. It wasn't easy preparing three meals a day for the two hundred residents that lived there. Mostly because the Little Sisters of the Poor fed and cared for their residents with whatever supplies were donated by local businesses as the Sisters made their way through the streets begging from one door to the next.

Marie and I were ten and eight years old respectively in 1965 when my mother volunteered us for the day. "You can lend a hand to the Little Sisters for a day. It will do you good to see how much you have to be grateful for in this world," she said.

So that morning long ago we rolled up our sleeves and broke a boatload of bread into bite sized pieces just as Sister Monique requested. By the end of the day we knew how to make bread pudding — enough to feed an army! And so it began.

Marie and I took to helping the Little Sisters in a big way. Their dedication and sincerity in caring for the residents did make us grateful for all we had and inspired us to become a part of their family. We always had fun, even doing chores. Can you imagine? When it was time to go home, we started looking forward to our next visit.

As the years passed, Marie and I continued to help on weekends and all through the summer months. By the time I was in the eighth grade we knew how to make soup by the gallon, fold sheets by the tonnage, shine the chrome on a wheel chair so you could see your face in it, and wax and buff a tile floor with prize-winning skill. The funny thing is, it never seemed like work. It always seemed like fun. The Little Sisters take great care to make sure their benefactors and volunteers understand their gratitude and feel their appreciation.

The residents looked forward to seeing us each week too and we enjoyed visiting with them. On holidays the Sisters planned sing-a-longs, picnics, and parties for the residents and their families. Often they enlisted us to put on plays to entertain them. There was always something to do, something to celebrate, something to enjoy, even if it was only sitting down to help a resident write a letter to a grandchild or friend.

When I turned seventeen, Marie told me she wanted join the religious order and become a Little Sister of the Poor. Then in January of 1975, my senior year in high school, she left home for the novitiate.

Leaving home is always bittersweet but she had opted for a religious vocation and one whose organizational rules prevented her from taking an active role in our family. She would be present in spirit, in contact by phone and through letters, but we would be permitted to see her only once a year. Whatever I had expected of our lives as adults, that wasn't it. But the choice wasn't mine to make. So we said good-bye and left the future in God's hands. And He has taken good care of us.

For the past forty years I have celebrated Thanksgiving, Christmas, Easter, and other holidays without sharing them with Marie — not even once. Vacations, my graduation, my wedding day, my birthday, her birthday, countless occasions of being sick, or sad, or worried about one thing or another all took place with me in my part of the world, and she in hers.

She has done the same, and survived breast cancer without me being physically present to comfort or support her. The life she chose placed a hefty price tag for two sisters who spent seventeen years hip-to-hip. But no vocation is ever easy. We each took our own path and have found joy and contentment with miles and miles between us.

All those years of separation might have pushed us farther apart, but God made sure that didn't happen, and we are grateful. In the early years when we were left to communicating only by letter, with a smattering of phone calls, we made the best of it. We shared happy occasions through photos and written descriptions of the events; the mailman also delivered our worries and woes to each other. It took effort but, it was all we had and we were worth it to each other.

Now, emails and smart phones keep us connected instantly. Isn't technology just grand?

Marie and I started out "helping the Sisters" for one day at my mother's urging fifty years ago. It led my sister to a lifetime of service to others, which has brought her great joy. Along the way, no matter how many miles came between us, we learned that staying close was worth the effort. We have seen much less of each other over the years than most sisters, but because of that, we appreciate each other very much. We celebrate and cherish each moment we are blessed to spend in each other's company.

Annmarie B. Tait

35

Loving Moments with Jesus

While most of the world is still quiet I wake up to Jesus and fellowship with Him amid the silence. For me the early mornings are the best time to sit before the Lord in quiet meditation. As daylight peeks through the windows or from behind the shades I begin my day in God's presence.

Solitude and quiet reflection never fail to bring me near to God. The Holy Spirit is key in helping me focus and stay free from distractions. Some days I come into God's presence with quiet thanksgiving and praise. Other days a song ushers me into His presence such as, "I Come to the Garden Alone." As the song says, we fellowship together, Jesus and me. Sometimes in quiet stillness and sometimes with soft music in the background. Those loving moments are precious because I can hear God clearer in the silence. He has my complete attention.

As I sit at Jesus' feet I am reminded of the story the Gospel writers record of Mary giving loving attention to Jesus. She anointed Him by pouring a very expensive ointment, spikenard, over his feet and wiped them with her hair. It was so lavished on Jesus that the whole house was perfumed.

Mary was criticized for her expression of love and gratitude to Jesus. Judas called it wasteful and thought the ointment should have been sold and given to the poor instead. But Jesus spoke up for Mary because her action had significance far beyond her understanding. Jesus told them Mary had anointed him for his burial.

Customarily Jewish women did not let their hair down in public but Mary's boldness and extravagance proved her strength. She was a devoted disciple of Jesus and out of love and gratitude she offered Him a gift.

On a prior visit to the home of Mary, her sister, Martha, and brother, Lazarus, Mary showed her devotion to Jesus by sitting at His feet listening to Him while Martha served. There was something about those loving moments with Jesus that drew Mary to him. When Martha complained to Jesus, He said Mary's decision to enjoy his company was the most appropriate response at the time.

The busyness of *serving* God can become barriers to getting to *know* Him. Like Mary, I don't want to miss an opportunity to know Jesus. I look for ways to offer Him my devotion, my praise, my worship and gratitude. Spending time with Jesus reminds me that He is with me in good times and bad. The message I hear from my Master is, "Be still and know," and in the stillness of those loving moments I am transformed, refreshed, reenergized and confident that God is all sufficient.

Lenora McWhorter

36

A Lurch, a Bump, and a Surprise

Not even a ray of sunshine pierced the rain clouds.

I assumed the trip to Disney World with my parents and special friend, Alan, would be postponed.

After several phone calls, they decided to take our chances with the rain. Reluctantly, I agreed. They pointed out that despite the inclement weather, we could still enjoy Alan's sixty-seventh birthday meal at Epcot's German pavilion.

After dating for almost seven years, Alan and I knew a lot about each other. As always, he arrived at my house exactly on time. However, wearing a jacket, especially in May, was out of character for him. He quickly explained he wanted protection from the possible rain.

Lines formed at the entrance to Disney's Animal Kingdom before we arrived. My parents waited for us near the turnstiles. Because of his Disney employee benefit, my dad provided free admission into the park for our group.

"We'll meet you at Epcot for lunch," my dad said as soon as we passed through the gate. It seemed strange to me. We usually enjoyed the parks together.

"Don't you want to stay and see the animals?" I asked.

Alan quickly intervened. "We'll meet you at the German pavilion for lunch." *Why did he dismiss my parents so quickly?* He hurried me past strolling tourists to his destination at the back of the park. A brief wait gave me time to catch my breath.

The attendant motioned to us. "Enter row one."

Obediently, I climbed into the safari jeep right behind the driver. Even though we had been on the ride several times, each experience was different. The number and types of animals roaming, lounging, and eating varied with the weather and time of day. With an early departure, we hoped to observe numerous animals in the African habitat.

Slivers of sunlight peeked through the clouds. The day warmed with no trace of rain. Surprisingly, even as the sun came out, Alan did not take off his jacket. Passengers filled each seat of the large vehicle. While Alan ignored me and talked to the honeymoon couple seated next to him, I watched other tourists.

With a lurch and bump, the truck began transporting us from Florida to Africa. We followed the rutted, dirt road up and down through the jungle. Around a bend hippos gathered in a pond. Their massive backs rose from the dark water. Tiny ears jutted from immense heads. Lounging at the shoreline of another pond, fierce looking alligators displayed sharp teeth ready to snatch intruders. Pink flamingoes balanced on single legs in the shallows of another small lake.

A rickety bridge swayed with the weight of our vehicle as water washed over the tires. We rumbled up a slight hill just in time to escape the rising flood. Dense jungle opened to a wide plain. Giraffes ambled among the trees. Their babies struggled to reach high leaves. Zebras grazed on brown grasses. Lions lounged in the shade on a high cliff. That area of the attraction always reminded us of our actual trips to Africa — several for Alan but only one for me.

Our driver continued his commentary about the wildlife as we observed the recreated African savannah. As the truck jerked forward, Alan slid to the floor.

With alarm, I looked down at him and noticed his unusual position. He was on one knee at my feet. From his jacket, he pulled out a black, velvet box. Looking deeply into my eyes, he asked, "Will you marry me?"

My heart pounded. My mouth went dry. *Was this a dream?* "Yes." I replied. "Yes, I will!"

After a quick kiss, he returned to his seat beside me. Passengers around us applauded. We gazed at each other and beamed. During our intimate drama, the driver had continued his normal monologue, oblivious to what was going on behind him. After the clapping subsided, a fellow traveler explained the surprise proposal.

For the rest of the ride, my gaze bounced back and forth from Alan to the glittering diamond on my finger. After almost seven years of dating, we were finally getting married.

Our official announcement came at the end of the ride. Over the loudspeaker, the driver informed everyone in that area of Animal Kingdom about our engagement during the ride. Visitors and employees offered smiles, best wishes, and congratulations.

I pulled out my phone and called my parents. "Alan and I just got engaged."

"We already knew about it," my mom said with a smile in her voice. "You were the only one who didn't know."

Reality set in. Puzzle pieces began fitting together. Alan's jacket hid the ring box. My parents' quick exit gave us time alone. Alan talked to the honeymooning couple so they would know what was going to happen. As he and my parents worked out the details, I almost ruined the surprise by wanting to postpone the excursion to a better time. But, the day turned our perfectly.

Later, Alan told me about the setting for his dream proposal. We would float in a hot air balloon over the Serengeti Plain of Africa above zebras, giraffes, gazelles, lions, and hippos. Flocks of native birds would be flying along with us. Disney's version of the African plains provided a delightful, memorable substitute.

Alan carefully planned a special African proposal for a couple of slightly-senior citizens. Love and romance aren't just for the young.

Rebecca Carpenter

37
The Locket

My twenty-fifth birthday would be the first one away from my family who always made birthdays special.

I was raised by older parents who looked at their children as God's gifts, and made each of us feel we were precious in God's eyes. They always made sure birthdays were wonderful for my brothers, sister and me. Each year we looked forward to a cake or card and a gift. No matter how scarce finances were, we knew we would get something for our birthday. It seemed to me, that because I was the youngest, my parents went out of their way each year when my birthday arrived.

After I was married, my husband, Jim, knew how I treasured each birthday and he tried to make them as set apart as my parents had. By the time we had been married five years, each birthday had been memorable.

This particular year would be different for us. We had finished Bible College and recently moved to our first pastorate in the northern California mountains. Our church was a home missions church, which meant the congregation was not able to support us but only provided us with a small home and the cost of utilities. Because of this, Jim had to work for our salary. We lived in potato country, so Jim had found part time employment in the potato cellars. That year, because severe weather he had not worked many hours and money was scarce.

But when my birthday arrived, a beautifully wrapped gift sat on the kitchen counter. I stared at the gift and Jim said, "Honey, here is your birthday present."

Tears gathered in my eyes and with a question in my mind of how he managed to afford this gift, I hugged the gift close. "But how did you do it?" I asked.

"It's a real miracle," he said, and then he told me the story of what had happened.

Knowing how much birthdays meant to me, and as my birthday approached, he began to pray that God would provide something special. Jim didn't know how God would provide but had strong faith that somehow it would be a memorable day.

While on an errand in a nearby town and walking down the street, he looked down at the sidewalk. Lying among the leaves was a twenty-dollar bill. He glanced around to see if anyone had dropped it. The streets were deserted. He picked up the bill and began thanking God for such a special answer to his prayer. He immediately knew what he would do with the twenty dollars.

Looking through the shop windows as he walked by, he spotted some lockets in the display case. One small silver locket caught his eye. He knew how much I loved jewelry and knew it would be the perfect birthday gift. He went in, and to his surprise, the little silver locket was one he could now afford. He picked out a card and paid a few dollars more to have the locket gift-wrapped. He brought his gift home and hid it until my birthday arrived.

As I opened the gift, I was surprised to see such a beautiful little locket. I realized that this was indeed a true miracle; not only did I get a lovely gift but Jim had enough money left over to buy a small cake.

The scripture, Jeremiah 31:3 (NIV) came to mind: I have loved you with an everlasting love. Some may say this incident was just a coincidence, but I knew with Jim's faith and love for me and a Heavenly Father who also loved me, He could make anything possible.

I thought back to all the birthdays I had and as I held the little locket in my hand, realized that God had wanted to bring a smile to one of his children on her special day.

Beverly Hill McKinney

38

Loved!

"Hi, Elsie! How are you? It's so good to see you!"

Janet greeted me as I entered the grocery store. Then she gave me a warm hug. Janet and I had been in the same Bible study group years ago, and in the few times I had seen her since, our exchanges had been casual.

Moments later, her husband appeared and greeted me as enthusiastically as Janet had. We chatted a bit and then continued on our separate ways. It all seemed rather strange and I found myself thinking, *I wonder what that was all about.*

Several days later at the same store, I met Marcia, a member of our church who usually greeted me with only a, "Hi." But this time she too, greeted me warmly and put her arm around my waist as we walked along. She even asked how things were going and seemed genuinely interested in my response.

After we parted to do our shopping, I began thinking, *It happened again — and so soon after the other time. What's going on?*

My mind was asking, "God, are you trying to tell me something through Janet and her husband, and now Marcia?"

Then I remembered.

Prior to these happenings, I had been feeling unloved by God — and people. Those feelings of not being loved gnawed away at me and I struggled to find assurance of God's love.

That was it! God had used his own unique way of involving his people to assure me I was loved by others, and especially by God Himself. There was no other explanation for the timing of these unusual happenings.

I'm thankful God assured me in a tangible way of his love at that time when I didn't *feel* it. But since then, I've learned that whether or not I *feel* his love, I can stand on the *fact* that God does love me because he tells me so in the Scriptures.

God tells me he lavishes great love on me — on all of us — and calls us his children.

First John 3:1 NLT says, "See how very much our heavenly Father loves us, for he allows us to be called his children, and we really are!"

Then the well-known verse in John 3:16(NIV) tells us God so loved the world that he gave his one and only Son, so that everyone who believes in him will not perish but have eternal life.

We are loved!

Elsie H. Brunk

39
The Most Excellent Way

Valentine's Day has come and gone. But love is always worth thinking about.

" 'Til death do us part." We're all familiar with that phrase. It's repeated in the marriage vows of thousands of people each year. It's a vow, and a hope, and sometimes a wistful wish. Unfortunately, statistics tell us the majority of marriages don't see the fulfillment of that vow. For many the hope of growing old with their partner is crushed in the early years of their relationship. For many more, the wistful wish turns to a bitter memory. Holding on to love, it seems, is hard.

The uncertain climate of love in today's society can be attributed to many things but it always comes down to a common denominator — people — ordinary, everyday people who have flaws and issues and self-centered tendencies. We are, in many ways, a hard people — hard on ourselves and hard on others. We're not prone to forgiveness or compassion or empathy. It's so much easier to walk away, walk by…and we're very good at convincing ourselves that's okay. Everyone does it; everyone expects it.

But Paul has said he will show us a most excellent way (1 Corinthians 12:31 NIV). First Corinthians 13 goes on to tell us what it looks like:

If I speak in the tongues of men and of angels, but have not love, I am only a resounding gong or a clanging cymbal. If I have the gift of prophecy and can fathom all mysteries and all knowledge, and if I have a faith that can move mountains but have not love, I am nothing. If I give all I possess to the poor and surrender my body to the flames, but have not love, I gain nothing. Love is patient, love is kind. It does not envy, it does not boast, it is not proud. It is not rude, it is not self-seeking, it is not easily angered, it keeps no record of wrongs. Love does not delight in evil but rejoices with the truth. It always protects, always trusts, always hopes, always perseveres. Love never fails.

1 Corinthians 13:1-8 NIV

A most excellent way, indeed, but how can we, who are so inclined to do the opposite, ever accomplish such love? We are all like trees planted in a desert, unable to thrive but, in Psalm 1:3 (NIV) Scripture tells us, we can be trees planted by streams of water, which yields its fruit in season and whose leaf does not wither.

If we draw from the source of love itself, we can and will love truly. That source is Jesus Christ. And His way is, indeed, most excellent.

Marcia Lee Laycock

40

A Love So Unlikely

"Y ou wouldn't be so lonely if you sang in the choir," Jo said gently. After the church service, she had made a straight line from the choir loft to where I sat, alone and miserable.

"That's probably true," I agreed. "I certainly don't like sitting here by myself. When do you practice?"

"Every Wednesday at 7:30, after Bible study."

"Okay, maybe I'll be there this week," I said, as I thanked her for the invitation. I didn't know Jo very well, as a matter of fact, I didn't know anyone very well. I hadn't been a member quite a year yet, and those 11 months had been filled with taking care of my husband. We had been looking for a church home when he received a cancer diagnosis, and West Hendersonville Baptist became the perfect fit. We attended church services when we could, but his health kept us from becoming too involved. Thankfully, Pastor Charles Magnet visited us often with his uplifting prayers and sweet fellowship, which ministered to our hurting hearts.

Arie had a sarcoma in his upper left arm, MFH, malignant fibrous histiocytoma, which he fought valiantly with chemotherapy, surgery, and radiation. In the end, the cancer may have won the battle, but the victory belonged to Arie's faith in Jesus Christ. After thirty-seven years of marriage, my husband went to his heavenly home.

I rejoiced in that truth. Nevertheless, my own life stretched before me — long, lonely, and uncertain. The Lord spoke to my heart, urging me to cling to Him, to not be afraid to go forward. I was to place my hope and future in His will and purpose for my life. In Him I would find a way to handle the loneliness and sorrow.

In obedience to the Lord's exhortation to "go forward unafraid," I went to church the day after my husband's service. I felt strongly that I was not to stay home, grieving by myself. I got up early, having decided to attend Sunday school, as well. I approached the door to the classroom, my stomach churning, and awkwardly entered the mostly-couples class. Quickly, I sat in the empty chair next to a kindly looking older lady. She introduced her husband and herself as Fred and Avis. When she lovingly held my hand during the prayer time, she instantly became my friend. I chose this class because the teacher was considered excellent and thorough, and indeed Helen was. The morning was off to a good start.

The church service that followed, however, was another matter. Sitting alone was painfully difficult with my husband no longer by my side. I was wretched and discouraged, and no doubt my expression and demeanor telegraphed my feelings.

As I gathered my belongings to leave, I saw Jo make her way toward me. She stopped by my pew and quietly made her observation and invited me to sing with the choir. Her kind words resonated deeply within, and I felt, again, the Lord urging me to "go forward unafraid." So when Wednesday arrived, a week after Arie died, I went to the rehearsal and joined.

I made that decision, never anticipating it would change the course of my life. I didn't consider my decision momentous, rather instead a reasonable way for me to avoid sitting alone in the congregation, with some enjoyment thrown in. After all, I did like to sing.

Avis was also in the choir, so I sat next to her, both of us excited about our budding friendship. Jo and others welcomed me, as did the choir director, who seemed especially pleased I had come. I settled in with an anthem to practice and a step forward out of the gloom of loss and grief.

It was a beginning.

Over the months ahead, unbidden tears would sometimes surface when the lyrics and melody touched those heart memories I treasured. Overall, though, I found the music to be healing, and when the moments were too emotional, I simply raised my folder or hymnal a tad higher. In the congregation, my friend Shirley would nod in sympathy, her smile an encouragement.

Choir was fun and church now emotionally manageable, two bright spots as I struggled through the first year of widowhood. Once the first miserable anniversary had passed, a startling interest and awareness began brewing within me. I found myself not just listening and following the director's lead, but I was also observing him, curious about this humorous, talented person who loved the Lord and was, surprisingly, still single.

Even more compelling, I observed him watching me. Intriguing as this was, however, a large problem loomed over any future we might have together. This handsome individual was nineteen years younger than me, actually born the year I married my first husband, so any thoughts of romance were *quickly* dismissed. I mean, contemplating what would it be like when I was basically 80 years old and Patrick was only sixty made any thought of us as a couple *impossible*!

As the days and weeks unfolded, I discovered a confusing reality. Attraction for someone and God's plan for a person seeking His will are beyond human understanding. Our observation of each other was turning into thoughtful conversation, until finally there was the indication of a possible date. When that didn't occur, I felt a strong nudge to attend a single's event at another local church. I was clearly not to wait round. My mandate from the Lord was to "go forward unafraid," trusting Him, and I was determined to do that. Interestingly, part of the nudge was to also mention to Patrick that I would be attending this event.

Afterward, though, I was more frustrated than ever, with Saturday evening only fostering more thoughts about my choir director. It was a disheartening and lonely drive home. In hindsight, I should have known better. God is always at work in our lives, *always*, but He reveals His plan for us in His time, will, and way…and usually in a remarkable, only-He-could-do-it-way which could never be fathomed.

By then I was teaching a small Sunday school class, so the next morning as I stood at the doorway to greet my students, Patrick stopped and said, "I almost called you yesterday to see if you could go to a concert with me last night."

My quick reply was, "I would have gone."

That was the turning point. Later, Patrick did admit that my attending the singles' event was the nudge he needed from the Lord to realize he could lose me to someone else. He didn't want that to happen, *glorious thought*! Still, there was much to resolve. Although I'm fortunately blessed with youthful genes and have been a many-years devotee to sunscreen, hair dye, and exercise, I'm still aging. Also fortunately, his genetics include pre-mature graying and a disposition toward older people. So we actually fit together!

We started dating, our relationship undergirded with prayer and the desire for God's will for both our lives. As I would bring up my "what ifs" and concerns to the Lord, I was always assured that our age difference was not to matter.

Patrick received valuable counsel from his cousin, Gretchen, whose perfect insight was from the Word itself, "You're only given today. You don't know what the future holds, so don't miss out on love now because of a distant fear."

With a blessing from Patrick's dear, late parents, Jack and Helen, yes, my former Sunday school teacher, and with Gretchen's biblical wisdom to provide clarity, our courtship advanced rapidly. We were married six months later in April, 2006, not quite two years after Arie's death. He would consider my marriage to Patrick an answer to his prayer for my life, and truly it is. To borrow a descriptive adage, Patrick and I are "two peas in a pod," our marriage a marvel in compatibility, contentment, and love, even after all these years.

In the end, we simply don't know our future or the length of our days on earth, but we are always commanded to go forward in faith, unafraid, trusting in the One who guides our way.

After Arie died, one of my dearest friends, Ernestine, sent me the verse from Isaiah 30:21 (NIV) which is still on my refrigerator door, a beacon of hope in 2004, a cornerstone of faith today:

> Whether you turn to the right or to the left,
> Your ears will hear a voice behind you, saying,
> "This is the way; walk in it."

Ann Greenleaf Wirtz

41

Red Fur and Freckles

"Never again! I never want another dog. It hurts too much to lose them."
I nodded in agreement at my husband's sad words. Seventeen years of doggie love laid to rest near the clothesline where Polly loved to sit left a gaping hole in our hearts. We know we can't protect ourselves from losing a family member or friend, but losing a dog, that's different. Dog ownership is voluntary. We won't make that mistake again.

We thought time would cure us from doggie love, but it didn't. We never stopped looking for that black nose poking through the door to greet us. Or the stub of a tail that wagged so hard it moved her whole rear end. Or the brown marble eyes that followed our every movement. I heard her tags jingle for months after she was gone, at odd times when the house was quiet. Sometimes I'd catch a glimpse of her on someone else's leash.

Two-and-a-half years later, we were set up. I've always heard that viruses come through email attachments. I should have known better than to open it, but there it was — a picture of a fluffy-eared redheaded cocker mix with a white stripe and freckles on his nose. I closed the attachment, but it was too late. I was infected.

"If you keep looking at the picture," my husband said after I opened it for the tenth time, "you're gonna fall in love with him."

"It's too late," I wailed. "I already have."

We adopted Winston on my birthday, 2007, from a rescue lady named Grace. A fitting name. *Grace. Grace. God's grace. Grace that is greater than all my fears.*

Like an eager suitor, Winston courted me. Like a tenderhearted schoolgirl, I fell in love.

His playful antics, so different from our dignified, first-born cocker girl, made me laugh aloud. Some days, for no reason at all, he'd race around the yard like Samson's foxes with their tails on fire. Every afternoon he'd pull my husband's socks off his feet, then shake them to death like a hunter with its prey. Other days he'd roll on the grass in joyful doggy abandon, tongue lolling in a happy doggy grin.

His zest for life never ceased. Every morning, sometimes before dawn, he'd climb from his nest by our bed and flap his ears so hard his tags rattled. It was his way of announcing to the world that morning had arrived. Racing from the room in search of his favorite toy, he'd pounce upon it with laser-like accuracy. Like the opening bell on the New York Stock Exchange, the resulting squeak would mark the beginning of our day.

His wholehearted love for his toys was fun to watch. He'd carry baby alligator, hot dog, and blue ball from room to room. We were never sure what was the criteria for being chosen as Toy of the Day, but he'd place the most-favored toy on the foot of our bed or on the couch, or he'd set it beside him at the door as he awaited our arrival at the end of the day. He bestowed the ToTD distinction on many of his toys, but red ball remained his favorite.

I'm sure I could have loved an ugly dog, but Winston's beauty captivated me. His soft, silky head and curly ears begged to be stroked. He'd often lie belly-up on our bed inviting us to scratch the snowy white fur of his chest and tummy. I'm not sure who enjoyed it more, him or me. There's something mighty powerful about petting a soft, warm puppy.

And then there was his tail. Because he was abandoned at the animal shelter as a sickly puppy, he missed the traditional tail docking many cockers endure. Long and red, with a strand of white at the tip, Winston's tail was, as Jo March said of her hair in the literary classic, *Little Women*, his "one true beauty." It never stopped waving, like a white flag of surrender after a long war.

Winston's adaptability fit my lifestyle perfectly. If I wanted to go for a walk, Winston was ready to go. Most times we'd walk our traditional route through the neighborhood, but our favorite path was around the lake. Delighted to be on the long leash, Winston would race ahead, sniffing at every tree. The only thing nicer than walking through that pine-scented forest in the springtime was sharing the walk with Winston.

Winston understood that a writer's life is often sedentary. If I spent the day working at my computer, he was okay with that. He'd gather his toys around him and stretch out on the floor, occasionally opening an eye to check my progress. He was patient and good.

It was a year of transition, that spring of 2007 when Winston inserted himself into my life. My eldest was graduating from homeschool high school and starting college. My youngest was growing more independent every day. Both had outgrown the frequent hugs and kisses I had so generously bestowed upon them in their younger years.

Winston, however, was an eager recipient of my affection. He never wiped his face in disgust after I planted a kiss on him. He willingly accepted every hug I enthusiastically shared. And often, during my early-morning quiet times, he'd cuddle close beside me on the bed and lay his soft head in the crook of my arm. Every now and then he'd release a sigh from deep within his doggy soul.

On Winston's last day, he did something he'd only seen in movies — he chased the neighborhood cat up a telephone pole. We'd walked together two days before, but that day was a workday for me. I left him sleeping in the sunny spot at the foot of my bed and headed out.

I knew something was wrong when I came home from lunch. No eager bark greeted me. No happily wagging tail. By dinnertime Winston was too weak to stand. A panicked trip to the emergency vet yielded a diagnosis I never expected to hear — multiple tumors, fluid around his heart, and no hope for recovery. By ten o'clock I had planted one last kiss on the soft fur of his nose and scratched his ears until he fell asleep.

"You're a good boy," I said. "Your mommy loves you. You've been a good friend."

Equally heartbroken, my husband repeated the words he'd said thirteen years earlier — "Never again. I never want another dog. It hurts too much to lose them."

But I know he'll change his mind. I will too. When the edges of our grief soften and the sweetest parts of doggy ownership begin to scratch again at the doors of our hearts, we'll open them up again.

Against our better judgment.

In the meantime, we're choosing to be thankful for the good and perfect gift God gave us in Winston. After all, only God would have thought to wrap love, loyalty, and laughter in red fur and freckles.

Every good and perfect gift is from above,
coming down from the Father of lights.
James 1:17 ESV

Lori Hatcher

42

The Gift

I sat up in bed startled. I looked around my bedroom to see what woke me. Suddenly everything came into focus. A door in my mind slammed shut on all the confusion and only one thought remained: *My dad is dying.* Realizing I'd made it through another night without a phone call, I sucked in a lungful of air. I'd been holding my breath.

After hurriedly dressing, I made my way to the care facility, greeted the familiar faces of the residents and walked to his room. This once comfortable atmosphere had become a place of fear, for I never knew if this might be the last time to visit my dad.

A shelf on the walls displayed pictures of his grandchildren. A few landscapes hung on the wall. A nightstand with a flat screen TV, on which he watched sports, sat in the corner. I stared at the piece of furniture that was set up in the room a week ago. A hospice bed replaced his twin bed.

My mom and sisters arrived a few minutes later and it seemed surreal as we chatted about weather, jobs…anything, but dad. That would make it too real. He lay on his back struggling for each breath. Our conversation seemed awkward and frustrating. But what were we supposed to do, or say?

His voice had commanded respect as a school administrator and successful football coach over a thirty-year career. His voice had sung songs of praise to God. His voice had given me the advice I needed and shared words of wisdom with his grandchildren.

But we'd had to become accustomed to his silence. Several months earlier, the combination of Parkinson's disease and severe dementia had left him unable to process thoughts. Once in a while, a moment of clarity surfaced, but he couldn't engage in conversation. I missed his voice.

Looking at my dad, I could hardly believe this was the man who had wrestled with me as a child and taught me how to throw a softball.

Dad, I miss you. As a child I went with you everywhere. I never wanted you to be alone. I always thought you seemed lonely. I believed with all the girls in our house, you didn't have anyone to be with. I'm so sorry I wasn't the boy you always wanted. I would have given anything to be the proud son you introduced to everyone, the one who played football — the star quarterback. I'm sorry I was the third girl — although I know you loved me. I would have loved to hear it just once.

I shook my head to clear the painful thoughts I rarely let surface.

My gaze fell again on the hospice bed. I watched him stare at the unseen, his mouth open, with a look of shock or surprise. I found it hard to continue. My stomach constricted with a knot of pain. For three days no change occurred. I watched his life ebb and flow with each breath.

The previous day I had done all I knew to do to help him know I was near. I read scripture, poems, and songs hour after hour. I wanted to somehow convey how I would miss his advice and just being able to talk to him.

"Dad, it's okay," I said. "I'm here. I'll watch mom and take care of her. It's okay to let go of this body. It's no use to you anymore. God will give you a new one. It's all right for you to go home now."

No response.

The afternoon became early evening. It was time to go. I walked toward him to say good-bye and give him a kiss on the forehead.

No! Wait. Don't say it. I don't want you to go, please! I want my daddy back. The one before disease took his mind. I want to have long talks and ask for advice about life and children I want more! Do you know, Dad, just how much you mean to me? What I am going to do without you?

Tears rolled down my face and soaked my shirt. I wiped my eyes and reached the railing of the bed. Leaning over, I gazed into his eyes that seemed to look through me.

"I love you, Dad," I choked out. I started to turn and leave. But he seemed to be staring at me in a different way. Could it be possible? Several days had gone by without the slightest recognition. Then his dry, cracked lips moved ever so slightly. In utter bewilderment and fascination, I stared. Time stood still. His arm moved. It wasn't the muscle-toned arm of my youth, but only skin and bone. He reached higher. I felt the gentle pats on my back.

Could this be happening? Did he touch me?

At the same time, his lips moved ever so slowly and he whispered, "I love you, too."

What just happened? My heart quickened. Did he say he loved me? Yes, he did. I heard him say those words. *Oh thank you, Lord.* A peace washed over me.

My dad, on the brink of death, with no food and only small sponge-soaked drops of water, patted my back and said he loved me. Those three words broke my heart. I only heard them a handful of times growing up. The realization of his whispered words hit me to the core. Although a wonderful dad, words of affirmation never came easy. As a child, I longed for his approval, and that continued throughout my adult life. Now, at age 55, I received it.

I left the room as quickly as I could without another word to my family. I knew what God gave me, and as I sat in my jeep and attempted to collect my thoughts, I looked up to the heavens. "Thank you for that gift," I whispered to my Lord.

I drove home. The scene replayed over and over. It occurred many times to me in the future.

Never again did my dad show a hint of recognition to anyone. He passed into glory two days later. God gave him the strength to put his arm around me, to look into my eyes, and say those precious words.

I may never understand how it happened, but I do know God is a God of miracles and the little girl who always sought her dad's approval and love received a gift that day. A gift which cast away the insecurities and doubts about her daddy's love.

Dianna Good

43

A Lifetime of Love

We've heard of "matches made in heaven." This was one, and it kindled a flame that endured through the decades. Neither Mildred nor I suspected the forces bringing us together.

In the summer of 1946, when I worked at a Baptist assembly in North Carolina, I dated a girl four years older than I was, Mildred's older sister. (I was 16 then.) Working there the next summer, I dated (among others) her next older sister, only a year older than I.

Then something odd happened. My parents moved to Northeast Mississippi to teach at a small college in the town where these girls lived. Nothing much happened for a while. The military draft resumed in 1948 and I was whisked off for a year in the Army. Then I returned and renewed my college education at Ole Miss, some thirty miles from our family's new home.

But at home during spring break in 1950 I met up with that second sister, who was accompanied by a yet younger sister named Mildred. The three of us hiked out to one of the renowned sites outside of town. Nothing notable about that. But during the hike I teased Mildred and she teased right back, going me one better at every turn. She had spunk, and she was quick. I made a pun and she came right back with a better one. She smiled and her eyes flashed. Better yet, I learned she was only two years younger than I (I was twenty by then) rather than the four I'd originally thought. That meant she was not off limits for dating.

The Korean War began that summer, but I was deferred by being in senior ROTC. When Mildred entered college that fall we dated every now and then when I was home from Ole Miss. She made lively conversation on substantive subjects, and we enjoyed long talks over coffee in various cafes. By Christmas I knew she was The One, but I didn't want to rush her. And by then she'd let me know she enjoyed my company.

In January I came home between semesters, and she stayed at the college to work. Then came one of the worst snows that region had ever known. Power lines snapped and roads were closed. We were snowbound. For more than a week we were gloriously trapped in a winter wonderland without outside contacts. So we were together morning and afternoon as well as dating in the evenings. The snow was one miracle, the fact that we never tired of our companionship was another. By the time the snow melted (honest, no help from us), we'd shared our first kiss and were engaged.

We had a long engagement because I couldn't support a family until I graduated. That gave us time to assure the certainty of our love. When I was commissioned through ROTC and graduated, the Army recalled me for the Korean War. We married — a small, simple wedding — and had five months together before I shipped out for Korea. We had a glorious reunion upon my return and embarked together on an Army career.

I'd been at outs with the church for some years, but Mildred's quiet faith slowly led me back in. Through the years, she was the strength that held our family together (four children by the time Vietnam occurred) during a variety of assignments and geographical moves. She did it all with a softness that made her a favorite wherever we went. She also taught both me and the children the importance of a prayer life.

After Army, she saw me through graduate school and became the ideal professor's wife. Students flocked to her as a surrogate mother and mentor. But finally we retired together, and for two decades then we had what we'd always wanted: unlimited time together, as we'd had briefly during that snow-enchanted courtship.

In our marriage we had never quarreled: we agreed at the beginning that when something went wrong between us we'd hold our fire and talk it out rationally after the emotions subsided. We did have disagreements, but talked in calm until we found workable solutions. Neither of us could stand to hurt the other one.

I've tried, vainly, to capture her quality in poetry. Only once did I come close:

> She speaks in trust that only grace allows,
> Modestly unaware her softness, strong —
> Stronger than stone or steel — holds up this house
> In love, to let the house hold up the sky.

We were lovers through sixty-one years, seven months and four days, until her long battle with ovarian cancer ended. She never complained, and she never doubted where she was going. Nor do I doubt where I'm going when the Lord calls. As I wrote in another poem, at the trumpet's call we'll

> ...wake to the Promise.
> There in that golden time
> We'll walk together with many millions more
> Into the daylight of eternity.

Donn Taylor

44

Winging It

Ready to spread his wings and fly, my first-born son was on his way to college. As my friend and my rock, he was always sensitive to my joys, my tears and my thoughts. I stood still as I watched him about to pull away from me in his Mustang that was loaded to the hilt with all his earthly belongings. I felt the urge to slip into the trunk, close the lid and go with him.

How will he manage without me? Will his laundry get done? Who will turn out the light when he falls asleep at his desk? Will he eat right? What if his alarm doesn't go off and he is late for his classes?

I suddenly realized that I had kept my son's wings folded far too long. He would fly. If a wing got caught on something now and then, it would be okay. It would mend. He would soar. And me…maybe it was time for me to dust off my own wings.

I took a deep breath, raised my hand in a weak wave, blew a kiss, turned my back and let loose the tears that strained to run down my cheeks. What had I just said to myself? Dust off my wings? Maybe I should try the vacuum instead.

The car pulled away.

I still had a daughter to raise. As time passed, I did a fair job wiggling my cleaner wings while I nurtured her to the stage of her flight. This time, it seemed much easier. Her wings already had nips and tucks in them. She had a strength that reeled from her strong will.

I had no doubt my daughter would conquer the world. Besides, her big brother came home to chauffer her to the same college he attended. She would be safe with him close by. They drove out of sight and my comfort level was high.

My wings vibrated with a new freedom. I remarried, and as empty nesters my husband and I looked forward to travel to new horizons (using an airplane of course!)

Oops! Life interrupted….

At forty-four years old, I delivered a daughter three months premature. She weighed one-pound nine-ounces. Well, let me tell you, my wings not only sagged during that trial, they seemed broken beyond repair. Doctors told us that our baby most likely would not survive.

But God's grace is amazing. Our daughter endured the impossible and she lived. She beat odds that seemed insurmountably unattainable. Later on, with sunlight in her heart and a sparkle in her eyes she too stretched her wings and flew into her own future. I know I worried more about this daughter, and still do, because today our world seems to be turned a bit upside down.

Now, I have two grown grandchildren who have flown on wings of confidence. I wondered if my daughter, their mother, had the same fears or expectations I had. I have another granddaughter who will, in a year, need to stretch her wings and fly. Since she is "the baby," I bet my daughter's heart will beat faster when she flies away.

More times than I can count, my wings have been mended from the injuries of life's many interruptions. They are now grey and frayed. Some injuries were easily fixed with tweezers; others needed rolls of duct tape; some, the super glue of righteousness!

Without my own freedom to fly, I couldn't have learned how to discern poor choices, foolish relationships, financial disasters, lost morals and the long list of trials I needed to face. Taking flight is a necessity for our children.

I'm not ready, quite yet, to fold my wings and take my final flight. But, I wonder at seventy-two years of age…should I get the vacuum out of the closet or should I just *wing it* from this point on? A mother's love puts all sorts of restrictions on our wings.

Alice Klies

45

A Lesson in Love

I adopted my children for all the wrong reasons. That's not to say that adopting them was wrong — just that my reasoning was wrong.

Growing up in a home where love was conditional, I always believed I had to earn my parents' love. When I was a young child, my parents kept foster children and in several cases they had tried to adopt. I believed if I did the things my parents had wanted to do but could not, I would earn their respect and their love. So, I proceeded to adopt.

Some people live vicariously through their children. I tried to live vicariously through my parents. Unconditional love was a concept I could not grasp. I had not experienced it and often felt I did not have the depth of love needed to parent my two children. At times, I believed my children would have been better off adopted by someone who had more love to give, who could hurt when they hurt, who could suffer through life's lessons with them. I struggled with the inadequacies of my love and whether my decision to adopt was fair to my children.

As a consequence, I could not understand God's love. I knew about grace, but could not personalize God's love for me — a sinner, blemished and tarnished by the world, unworthy of Jesus' death on the cross. No matter how hard I tried to be good enough to earn God's favor, I fell short.

Then came Kurtis.

Still trying to earn my parents' approval, I adopted Kurtis when he was twenty-three months old. At that time, he was the most severely abused child to survive in the United States. He had been placed on hot stove burners, dipped in scalding water and hit over the head with a chair. Developmentally, Kurtis functioned at the level of a nine-month-old.

A more beautiful child than Kurtis had never been born. His hair was the color of Rumplestiltskin's spun gold, his eyes the color of honey, the skin on his face was soft and smooth as cream. Beyond the handsome features was a child who was behind in every area. His clothing covered the hard lumps of scar tissue on his buttocks and the withered and deformed left leg.

The challenge was to get Kurtis to function at his maximum potential. I turned the living room of our small country home into a gymnasium. Balls of every size, blocks, tilt boards, sand and water tables replaced my antique living room furniture. Each activity was planned to stimulate some aspect of his development. Surgeries were scheduled for the foot, the legs and the eyes. He took part in physical, occupational and speech therapy. He attended an infant-toddler stimulation program. No need was left unmet.

Kurtis and I became well known at our rural community hospital. For every surgery, Kurtis held hands with one of the nurses and walked bravely into the operating room. This was the second attempt to surgically straighten his eyes. With Kurtis out of the room, I sat and waited, prayed and waited, paced and waited.

In the small green-gray hospital room with the faded lime and orange striped curtains that separated the beds, I watched the clock with the slow moving hands. Looking out the window I could see the life flight helicopter flying over the treetops as it approached, then watched as it landed and lifted from the pad outside this wing of the hospital. Kurtis loved the helicopters. Too bad his eyes would be bandaged when he came back to his room. I moved from the window to the big green foldout chair where I had spent a sleepless night. I continued to sit and wait.

Eventually, I recognized the sound of Kurtis' hospital crib being wheeled down the hall. I pressed myself against the wall to allow room for the nurses to roll it into place. There was my Kurtis — peaceful, still, and so very small. Bulky squares of gauze had been taped over both eyes with the surgical tape forming an X across the tiny bridge of his nose. Even now he was beautiful, but oh, so fragile.

"You can hold him if you'd like," the nurse called over her shoulder as she left the room.

Kurtis slowly awakened from the anesthetic and began to whimper. I lowered the side of the crib, took him in my arms and carried him to the big green chair. Holding him against my chest, I could smell the sterile odors of surgery on him. As he continued rousing from the drug-induced stupor, his whimpering became a cry. Tears seeped from under the gauze bandages and rolled down his cheeks. These were not just any tears, but tears of blood, streaking down his face and onto his chin where they mingled with the tears that were now washing down my own cheeks.

I suddenly became aware of my own discomfort. My eyes hurt — really hurt! My own salty tears were burning and stinging. For the first time, I experienced pain when my child suffered.

I had been praying for a deeper understanding of God's love and a reassurance that my love for my children was genuine and unconditional. Now I knew I had not suffered with my children, because my children had been mercifully spared anguish. As I watched the blood flow down Kurtis' cheeks I knew for the first time how much God loved me. If I could suffer this much watching Kurtis, how must God have suffered as he watched his Son, Jesus, bleed and die on the cross for me?

God had used my wrong reasons for adopting and taught me one of life's most important lessons which is how to measure love, His and mine.

Mason K Brown

46

Giving...
The Unforgettable Gift

*A crowd is not company; and faces are but a gallery of pictures;
and talk but a tinkling cymbal, where there is no love.*

Francis Bacon

We were college students when my husband and I first noticed each other in church. I sang in the choir and Bob played his trumpet in the orchestra. Mine was not the most outstanding voice in the choir, contrary to the sounds that came from his most cherished horn, which I later learned he had played since he was in the fifth grade.

Our college Sunday school class retreat was held in Yosemite National Park that year. That is where we shared our first moments together...amidst the casual atmosphere and comfortable laughter of close friends. The exchange of a few glances, along with some minute bantering, ignited an eternal flame of devotion that has remained unquenchable.

This occurred over forty-eight years ago. Bob was a second-lieutenant in the midst of a transition from the Army National Guard into the U.S. Army, which meant he would soon be forced into temporarily relinquishing the pursuit of his college degree in order to attend helicopter flight training as a medical evacuation pilot. Concurrently, his job — building saunas for a manufacturer — phased out while he awaited orders that would provide the path toward our future.

During this overlapping of obligations, we were engaged to be married in March of 1969. Despite the forthcoming orders and lack of a job, Bob surprised me with a sparkling, one-carat, diamond engagement ring which I assumed took most, if not all, of his life savings. At Christmas, I was also shocked to receive a beautiful suede leather coat with a genuine mink collar.

Needless to say, these lavish gifts were wonderful but I was more enraptured by the thoughtful personality of this officer and gentleman who had stolen my heart.

Soon after our marriage, Bob served a year in Vietnam. Then we were off to his next assignment in West Germany where our only child was born.

Life couldn't be sweeter and I have such a wonderful husband, I thought, as I counted my blessings on the way home from church one Sunday evening near Landstuhl. As I quietly reminisced in the car over earlier days — me in the choir and Bob in the orchestra — it suddenly occurred to me that during all of our moving I had not seen Bob's trumpet among our household goods.

"Bob, where's your trumpet?" I asked.

There was silence.

"Bob, your trumpet. Where is it?" If it hadn't been in our household goods when they were unpacked in Germany, where could it be?

Sheepishly, he answered me with a question. "Do you remember that suede coat I gave you the Christmas before I left for flight school?"

"Yes."

"Well, I hocked my trumpet to get you that coat."

I couldn't believe it. Tears coursed down my cheeks as we continued our drive home. I was humbled by this revelation. My thoughts resumed the counting of my blessings. The greatest one I had received was Bob's giving a gift from the heart.

The coat has disappeared into never-never land. However, I will *never* forget what was given through the precious, selfless and silent "giving" of his unforgettable gift of love.

Phyllis A. Robeson

47

Rescued by Love

Y ou've got to come down here," my granddaughter, Savannah, said over the phone. "We have the perfect dog for you."

"Who's we?" I asked.

"Celeste, Emily, and I. It's a rescue dog. Hurry."

Well, they are my teenage grandchildren, so I decided to accommodate them, all the while feeling that I wasn't sure I wanted another dog.

The last one I had was a fifty-pound black chow with a purple tongue who decided to bite a lab and took me for runs when I was only trying to walk him. He wasn't the cuddly type! The only thing he apparently feared was going up and down stairs. When there was a tornado alert and we retired to the basement, he stayed upstairs, braving the storm. He wouldn't do the stairs even when it was sunshiny, nor when offered a treat.

So, after he "retired," I'd made it clear my next dog would be calm, love me, and let me be the boss.

Reminding myself that these were the grandchildren who *made* me get a cat at a time I was more a dog person, I nevertheless met them outside the store where there were cages filled with pleading, rescued dogs.

Nope! None appealed to me except for the fact I wished they all could find good homes, but not mine. Then…the girls saw me, ran to me with wide smiling eyes and mouths and steered me to a back cage.

The cage was opened and there was the most beautiful ball of long blond and white fur. It's big brown eyes pleaded with me to be kind, and of course I was as I led *my* Pomeranian along the sidewalk for a while, although that wasn't necessary. I knew he was mine.

I did ask if they'd take fifty dollars less than the asking price, although I would have bought him for fifty dollars more, even if I had to sell my car to do it. The rescue group *happens* to have their business right outside Tractor Supply so naturally the five of us (me, three granddaughters, and my pom) went inside to purchase all the necessities such a regal Pomeranian requires. I was thinking… maybe I *will* have to sell my car.

But…what can you do when it's love at first sight?

We debated the name for such a regal male member of our family who turned out to be whiter and lighter blond after a bath. The rescuers said his name was Bandit, but that didn't seem to fit. At least not until one day when I left half a sandwich on the coffee table while I went out to get the mail. Then, I understood why someone had named him Bandit.

During our naming however, I chose Rigel, which was the name of a black Newfoundland who survived the sunken *Titanic*. He swam for three hours, barking to alert the lifeboat occupants and the rescuing ship, *Carpathia*. An officer on the ship became that Rigel's master.

My Rigel was a survivor too, although of what, I don't know. But he also represented my fiftieth novel, *Hearts that Survive — A Novel of the Titanic* that became the survival of my writing career at a time when so many changes were taking place in publishing and I was without a book contract for the first time in thirty years.

Depression threatened me, until I saw the Bible verse, "Show me the wonders of your great love," and decided to ask and allow the Lord to show me if he wanted me to continue in the career he led me into. He did show me and that turned out to be my miracle book.

Sometimes when I'm signing that book (several times a year at the Titanic Museum in Pigeon Forge, Tennessee), someone who doesn't know or think about the *Titanic* having sunk in 1912, will ask if I'm a survivor (at least…I think that's the reason they ask and not because I look to be over one hundred years old).

I say, "Yes, I'm a survivor, but not of the *Titanic*."

That's what I think about my life, (likely most of us have trials that we've survived), and Rigel's. We have a good life together. He's calm, takes me for walks, and most of all, he loves me and I love him.

And…I *say* I'm the boss, but…

Yvonne Lehman

48

A Lasting Lesson

Dad couldn't deal with handicapped individuals. He changed the subject when a special needs child became the topic of conversation. He never voiced it, but his actions and attitude spoke volumes. *If you don't talk about it, you don't need to recognize children born less than perfect.*

Ironically, I taught a class that included several handicapped children. Maybe his attitude is what made me so bent on helping them.

When I came home to visit, I hoped he'd see that they were no different than any other child. They laughed, they cried, they wished for special things, and they had likes and dislikes. But Dad didn't want to hear about the children. He abruptly changed the subject whenever I tried to tell a story about one of them.

When our first baby arrived shortly before Thanksgiving of 1966, our anticipation and joy turned to shock, for Julie was a spina bifida baby. Along with silver blonde hair, big blue eyes, and skin that shone like satin, she had an open spine and paralysis of her legs, bowel, and bladder.

My husband relayed the sad news to both sets of grandparents. The message we received from three of them showed hope and acceptance. My dad had nothing to say about his first granddaughter. He visited me in the hospital and pledged his support and love to me for rough times ahead. Sadly, his visit didn't include a peek into the nursery.

Within days, Julie became a patient of a well-known neurosurgeon at a children's hospital in Chicago. He closed the opening in her spine and inserted a shunt to drain fluid from her brain. It was so much to endure by one tiny soul. I wasn't able to stay with Julie, as a difficult delivery, a slow recuperation, and distance kept me at home where I agonized over our separation and spent a great deal of time in prayer.

My mother and I spent our phone calls talking about Julie. I tried to live with hope, but sometimes hope is a fragile entity. Mom's positive words buoyed me up when I occasionally fell into despair. I spoke to the nurses daily, and we went to visit our little girl every weekend. To us she was perfection.

One night during the second week, Dad called. "I went to see Julie today," he blurted before even saying hello. My heart skipped a beat, and I clenched the phone. Dad went on to describe all he'd seen at the hospital, how impressed he'd been, and how beautiful Julie looked. His voice quivered more than once as he talked to me. Tears flowed down my face at the knowledge that Dad was beginning to accept a handicapped grandchild. I knew how hard that visit had been for him.

That was the first of many such visits. Dad worked several blocks from the hospital, and he spent many of his lunch hours walking through the cold, rain, or snow to check on Julie's progress. His reports to me were descriptive and filled with love for both his daughter and granddaughter. I could detect a little more acceptance on his part with each visit.

One evening he called, and I noted excitement and pleasure in his voice as he told in great detail of seeing Julie receive a Christmas doll from a hospital auxiliary volunteer. The woman tied the tiny doll to Julie's isolette within her line of vision while dad watched. He described the doll from head to toe as well as the red satin ribbon used to fasten it. Those were words I needed to hear since I had not been present, words I came to treasure.

Dad's visits came to an end in the middle of January when Julie died. Despite our grief, I gave thanks that Dad had come to accept a less than perfect child as part of our family. Her time here was limited, but she taught him a lasting lesson, and the bond between my dad and me grew stronger than it had ever been.

A loving God worked yet another small miracle using a tiny soul who worked her way into her grandfather's heart, one short visit at a time

Nancy Julien Kopp

49

Rays of Love

Music is very dear to my heart. Over the years, God has ministered to me through songs. I enjoy singing, especially singing praises to Him. One Sunday, about a year after my husband and I began attending a new church, we sat behind the pastor's wife. After the service ended, she turned to me and said, "You have a beautiful voice. Why don't you sing on our worship team?"

Having never considered being a part of a worship team or singing from a stage, I was surprised and excited, but scared. As I began to sing with the worship team, I felt self-conscious. I was petrified my harmony would be off-key. Many times during the service, I held back singing into the microphone, fearful that my voice would make the rest of the group sound bad.

Soon after I started singing with the team, I noticed a couple, Jon and Susie, who sat near the front of the sanctuary on the right side. From the minute I laid eyes on Susie, I was drawn to her. She had an infectious smile and eyes that sparkled like jewels. Our eyes would connect, and I could feel God's love radiate from her to me. It filled me completely and then reflected back to the congregation through my voice. When feeling unsure of myself, I sought Susie's face and drew strength from her smile.

After the service was over, Jon walked onto the stage to shake our hands or give us hugs. He thanked each of us for leading the congregation in worship. That was always a special time for me and appreciated by the worship team. Jon and Susie usually didn't stay long after the service, and when they were not in their seats up front, I missed them dearly.

As months passed and I observed Jon and Susie, I thought they were the picture-perfect couple. I marveled at their obvious love for each other. They gazed with deep affection at one another like newlyweds. This intrigued me because they were an older couple. She and Jon held hands and touched each other in affectionate ways that emphasized a deep, mature love and respect for each other. It reminded me of the relationship Christ has with His bride — the church.

A year or so after I started singing, Jon was diagnosed with terminal cancer. Over the course of the next several months, Jon underwent various treatments. At times, the treatments made him very sick and weak. Yet when possible, he and Susie came to church and took their places at the front of the sanctuary. When communion time came, he somehow found the strength to stand and take communion with Susie. He knelt at the stage for prayer, and then made his way back to his seat, often with the help of someone by his side. Lying on the front row, Jon rested his head in Susie's lap for the remainder of the service. His desire to be with his church family and the importance of being surrounded by their love was of utmost importance to him. During this time, Susie stood faithfully by his side and supported him.

That spring, after Jon's death, Susie continued to attend church, sit in their place at the front of the sanctuary and radiate God's love through her smile and sparkly eyes.

It was an amazing journey for me to watch them from the stage. Through their actions they taught me so much about God's love. They taught me about unconditional love for each other and for God. They taught me about perseverance and dedication to their Savior. They taught me it's okay to be seen during our weak times, and it's all right to be scared. They taught me the value of letting the church family love and minister during times of need. But most of all, they taught me the value of being God's rays of love shining into the lives of others.

Through Jon and Susie's love, God shone into my life and gave me the courage to boldly sing for His glory.

Sheryl M. Baker

50

If Only by Toe-touch

Mother began her story, saying, "On a bone-marrow-freezing February day, I, a slim twelve-year-old girl who almost died of Brights Disease when I was seven and had to miss a year of school in the 1930's, heard Daddy say, "The boy's gone to hook up the mules to pull us out so we can get to the chapel." And within thirty minutes, there was the fourteen-year-old neighbor who lived in our cove driving Maude and Mandy down the slick rutted-out road, ready to hook up to the bumper of Daddy's Model-T that was stuck hub deep in brown mud.

"Peering out the back window, a hand resting on my seven-month-old baby brother's tiny casket that had been placed on the back seat between my sister — who was two years younger — and me, I never took my gaze off the wiry young boy with black hair who talked and clucked to his already overworked yet obedient mules. That day…was the day…I fell in love with your Daddy. And never stopped loving him."

"But I wasn't in love with your Mother," Daddy said, ears wiggling while his laughter filled the family room. "I thought she was too young for me. And when I received a letter during the war overseas from the cove in Alabama, a letter that was from her, I never answered her back."

"Can you believe that!" Mother added with an incredulous look.

The room filled with more laughter and disbelief as the fire crackled and popped in my parents' mountaintop home.

"Wasn't it good to get news from home?" I asked Daddy. Mother had always taught me to answer letters and to write thank you notes.

"Yes, it was good to get news from home," Dad replied. "The boys I soldiered with during World War II were always hungry for news. But I wasn't the best letter writer and was living in foxholes most of the time, jumping as a paratrooper behind enemy lines, and didn't take the time to write my own family often, much less shy little girls. I was dodging bullets and sometimes

I fought while sick with spine rattling flu. The doctors were ordered to give us an aspirin and send us back to the front lines. We were short on men and fearful the enemy would break through our lines. We sometimes lived in five feet of snow in forests crawling with the enemy. When I was off duty during a lull or when our commanding officers pulled us off the front line and shipped us back to England for a rest before the big push to end the war, I was interested in having fun dating the English girls more my age. I didn't think much about the girls back home. I lived for the moment for I might die in the next battle."

When Daddy arrived stateside, having survived four hellacious years in the European theatre fighting Hitler's war — with all but about five of the one hundred twenty-five men in his original Company I either buried in Europe or sent to other commands because of ankle and leg injuries from bad landing falls — he was bone thin, battle weary, and suffering from "battle fatigue" and nightmares. The term PTSD had yet to be adopted.

One thing Daddy knew. "I wanted to settle down and marry and have a family. I was tired of killing. I was tired of waking up at night reliving battles, dangerous river crossings, and beachhead landings where I lost some of my best men. I wanted to move forward with my life. I wanted to live. My family had moved to the city before I joined the Army but first thing I did when I arrived home from Germany was buy a car so I could drive back to the cove to visit the old folks and to ask about your mother's younger sister. She wasn't as shy as your mother. I was told she'd married. So I asked about your mother — I thought the world of her family — and was told she had moved to town as well, to find work in a drugstore."

Mother picked up the story from there. "I was painfully shy. A straight-A student but too shy to read an English paper in front of the class in high school. When the teacher asked me to read my work, I declined. The teacher said, "You can read your A-paper to the class or take an F. I whispered with downcast eyes, 'I'll take the F.'

"Of course the teacher didn't give me an F. He was only trying to pull me out of my shell. So one day, about five years later when the war had ended, when I looked up to see your daddy walking down the aisle of the drugstore

147

wearing his uniform, I couldn't believe my eyes. The boy I'd always dreamed about had returned home. And he had come to look me up — even though I was his second choice because I was the shy sister! We were married within two months. It took me a few years to become more outgoing, but I finally decided shy was no fun — and eventually did venture from my shell. Your Daddy was the only man for me.

"And I finally got the boy I saw through the back window of our Model T Ford on that frozen ground day when the only flowers blooming for a funeral were yellow jonquils that had managed to pop open despite the cold weather. Even though I'd lost one of the loves of my life — my little brother who was like my own child and the sweetest and happiest baby — and was on my way to his funeral, I'd found another love."

"And the rest is history," Daddy said. "When I flew back to the States after Germany surrendered and the Russian army poured in, your Mother and I had you three children, and here we are...still married like two peas in a pod."

But even I, with all this lovie-dovie talk, knew my parents' marriage hadn't always been easy. Mother shared one last important tidbit. "Even though we might have had the biggest argument during the day, our feet always touched at night when we slipped beneath the covers — even during the hot and humid nights. We never stopped being close, if only by toe-touch beneath the sheets."

An amazingly true two-peas-in-a-pod toe-touch love story.

But perhaps there was more. I'd often wondered about those two lovebirds. Mother almost died from a disease most never recovered from during the depression, when the doctors lived far beyond raging rivers that had yet to be tamed, and medicines were hard to find...if there was any money.

And then there was Daddy. Wounded once to receive a purple heart along with several other medals. He shouldn't have survived World War II when many paratroopers were killed in the sky — sitting ducks before landing — while others were taken out by land mines and machine gun nests. Daddy was frequently behind enemy lines or on the front lines facing tanks that tried to blow men from their foxholes or planes that strafed mountain-high tactical positions that were so steep, the wounded, bloodied and broken, had to be tied to rocks to keep them from rolling down Italy's mountains before medics

148

could arrive with stretchers during a battle lull. But somehow, for some reason, Daddy did survive when so many others failed to live to make it home.

Then years later, against all odds, I was born, the third child to a man who only wanted two children. When this realization finally dawned on me, that technically or by wishful thinking, I shouldn't have been born, I had an awakening. My soul and spirit had beaten several odds to make an appearance in the form of a human being, a body of clay, a temple for the Holy Spirit. And I could only deduce that I was here by God's grace, writing for him, telling tall tales and a few short ones, for a reason — acknowledging to others my life had meaning.

Yes, I'm here for a grander purpose in life, to glorify God with my writing and my life's testimony. Perhaps for my descendants. Perhaps for others who do not yet know Christ. And perhaps to bolster Christians who are world-weary and need to hear about the stories of others while striving to walk in the light, no matter how difficult the journey.

Having survived this cruel world so far, I pray that I do God and the story of his Only Son justice, as he guides me through this life of many trials. That I tell the stories that need to be told, humbly and truthfully, and in a way that God's Word comes alive so others may seek to know Christ, and live eternally.

And since my parents lived through horrendous atrocities and both experienced near death to "accidentally" bring me into such a wicked world full of sinful people who would persecute God's chosen ones, I must remember what Paul wrote in 1 Corinthians 10:31. Whatever you eat or drink or whatever you do, you must do all for the glory of God. (NLT)

Therefore, know this: We are *all* here for a purpose. I will continue to pray that those who read the *Moments* book series will be encouraged to seek their purpose in life. May God bless, and may God always be with you as you seek your higher calling and a closer relationship with the Lord. And may you always toe-touch with your loved one beneath the covers — until death do you part and God calls you home.

Vicki H. Moss

51

I Love You All the Much I Got

I pray that you, being rooted and established in love,
may have power, together with all the Lord's holy people,
to grasp how wide and long and high and deep is the love of Christ.

Ephesians 3:17-18 NIV

I don't think they get it — my kids, that is. We're a combined family. My husband has two sons and I have two…but they're all "our" boys. There's never been any separation in them to us — mine, yours. They're all the same. Still, I don't think they get just how much we love them.

Anytime my husband and I refer to our sons, it's our boys. When one son aches, both of us feel the pain. We've cried with and for one another when a child has experienced hardships. We've paced the floor throughout the night, and we've gone to our knees together, crying for God's protection and favor, healing, and provision for each of our boys. Yet they don't get it.

Despite how we stand in the wings waiting with our arms open, it takes our sons a long time to share their hurts with us. Pride, embarrassment, fear they'll disappoint us — it doesn't matter. They never seem to get that we love them despite their hardships or their successes. When our oldest was little, his favorite saying was, "I love you all the much I got." We love them wider than the widest ocean and deeper than the universe stretches — "all the much we got."

Sometimes it's hard to wrap our heads around God's love. Paul describes his prayer for our understanding better than anyone. Imagine just how wide, long, high, and deep the love of Christ is. My own eyes are not always open to God's longing love either. He shares this same love for me — and even greater, than what I share for my children.

Each Valentine's Day, I send all my boys a chocolate bunny. It's a simple, delectable reminder that we love them more than life itself. The love of a parent...the love of God, is deep. Deeper than we can understand at times, withstanding a multitude of wrongs against it.

I've begun telling God up front that I love Him. It's time I verbally and spiritually begin to step up to plate for the Father whose love is unending — whose love is wider and deeper than I can imagine.

Take time to tell God you love Him — "all the much you got."

Cindy Sproles

52

An Astonishment
of Unicorns

What do Men know?
Because they have seen no Unicorns for a while
does not mean we have all vanished.

Peter S. Beagle

Seven years ago when my husband, Ken, suggested I leave my job with
Peace Corps in Washington D.C. and retire to Northeast Washington
State, I whined, whimpered and wailed. Exchange work which included
international travel, a decent salary and the exciting hubbub of the nation's
capital for a sedentary life in the back of beyond?

But then my wily and thoughtful spouse promised me a rambling country
dream house with space for cats and dogs...and my unicorns. "We've never
been able to display much of your unicorn collection in the living room of
this townhouse," he pointed out. "And half my Don Quixote figurines are
still in their original boxes. We can spread everything out!"

His argument began to sway me. Lawns and gardens and wall space! I finally
agreed to the move. When we arrived at the country property, I delighted
that it boasted a stable. "We may never have a herd of horses," I said as we
surveyed the sturdy structure, "but if a unicorn happens by, we'll have a stall
to welcome it."

Ken shook his head and smiled. "I'd be astonished if one did."

Astonished? I perked up. Until that moment, my favorite collective noun
had been "an exaltation of larks." But, now...I quickly counted the stalls.
"We can house four," I announced. "We've a stable big enough for an entire
astonishment of unicorns."

Ken chuckled conspiratorially. "And room for Rosinante, as well, just in case Don Quixote ever drops by and seeks shelter for his steed."

As we walked back to the house, I wondered if we really had enough wall space and shelves inside for both my unicorns and Ken's collection of Quixote porcelain figurines, posters and paintings. "I can hardly wait to unpack our crates," I said, taking his hand.

My love affair with unicorns began when I was ten and read Lewis Carroll's *Alice Through the Looking Glass*. Alice had happened across one of the enchanted creatures taking a break from its endless struggle with its foe, a lion. Alice and the unicorn beheld one another with astonishment. The unicorn explained that it thought that children were mythical monsters, not really real. Alice admitted that she always had believed the same of unicorns.

"Well, now that we have seen each other," the unicorn said, "if you'll believe in me, I'll believe in you. Is that a bargain?" I remember nodding as I turned the page. I vowed then to forever believe in unicorns, and to shelter them whenever I could.

I have hunted unicorns at museums, The Cloisters in New York City and The Cluny in Paris. Each morning I sip tea from a gold-rimmed unicorn mug. My Christmas tree glitters with unicorn ornaments that I've collected from Thailand, Mongolia and Guyana. Should I ever get to Shangri-la or Saturn, I'd hope to cart one back from there.

During the decade I worked overseas with the Peace Corps, I carried my unicorn keychain with me from country to country. I would run my thumb across it for good luck while I opened doors to rented rooms, shared houses, and miniscule studios. And until I lost it in a burglary in Belize, I often wore a unicorn ring with a tiny ruby that my best friend gave me at the onset of my odyssey.

When I returned to the States in 1998, I discovered the opening world of the Internet. I eventually joined an online dating service, SocialNet, and through it met Ken. While we pursued our cross-country romance, I happened across a website, Neopets, a virtual pet community. I adopted a unicorn and named it Kennikorn. While Ken and I courted by e-mail and phone, separated by half a continent, I whiled away weekends at the library computer entering Kennikorn in games and battles. Ken listened while I described my mascot's prowess, and knew that romping online with Kennikorn helped quell my anxiety and soothe me through lonely times.

So we settled into the country house and Ken decorated it just the way he wanted, Quixotes and unicorns everywhere. A few years later, one Valentine's Day Ken was diagnosed with pancreatic cancer. He stayed home, just as he wanted, surrounded by his artwork and animals. He finally died on one gloomy June.

So now loneliness lurks again. Sometimes I gaze out the kitchen window across the pasture toward the empty stable, recollecting how in legend unicorns had been known to cure everything from gout to epilepsy. They also can neutralize poisons, maybe even such poisons of the spirit as despair. I've slowly moved from grief to reconciliation in this home we shared for a short five years.

When grief seems overwhelming, I head for the bookcase in the family room where three unicorn music boxes dwell. I wind up all three. My two snow globes tinkle out "Over the Rainbow" and "Dreamland," and the jewel box chimes in with "Camelot." Perfect songs about fantasy worlds. They play on for fifteen minutes, in a melodic counterpoint that never fails to lift my sagging spirits.

I find myself astonished at how quickly the music works its magic. My mood always shifts from gloom to gratitude, from despair to hope. I glance at Ken's "Man of La Mancha" Broadway posters and the playbill for Nureyev's "Don Quixote." Whatever the future holds, I remind myself, I will have the solace of the memory of our shared lives here, snug and safe. The walls and the shelves won't let me forget.

I still believe in unicorns and hope that Alice does, too.

Terri Elders

53
Love Knots

Is there anything else that ties the heart up in knots like love can?

I wondered about this statement many times when I first gazed into the eyes of my three children. I carefully pulled blankets aside to peer at every inch of their torsos. I counted each finger and toe. I pushed my face close to feel their breath against my cheeks. I chuckled as I watched their tiny lips smack together in search of nourishing milk. Love knots started to form; they threatened to play havoc in my heart.

I don't want to undermine the heartthrob or heartbreak of young love-puppy love or even mature love in adult marriages that can produce pain and tears, but the love knots that coil in a mother's heart have always plagued me as being unique.

I carried a precious baby seed within my womb for two of my children for the usual nine months. As the embryos grew inside me for each pregnancy, I began to feel a tingle, then a small bump or roll, and finally calisthenics with kicks and jabs that downright hurt. Sometimes the nauseous urge to empty my tummy during the first trimester overwhelmed me. My ankles disappeared and my body ballooned into someone I didn't recognize. Through it all, my heart knotted with a love that made it all worthwhile.

My third pregnancy at age forty-four lasted only twenty-seven weeks before I delivered my one-pound nine-ounce daughter. Love knots quadrupled and intensified. I felt cheated of my nine-month experience and three months visiting an intensive care unit gave me an angry, frustrated, broken, fearful love knot.

Knots tumbled with hope; they twisted with anxiety and then finally unfolded when wires and tubes were removed from my baby, when weight gain skyrocketed and announcements came that my baby girl might live.

I believe mothers are in an intricate dance of sorts with their children at conception. I think we are connected or even affected emotionally by hormonal behavior of each other. After all, we share the same food and drink…maybe even the same feelings. We are one. How can this possibility not make our love for our children more intense?

When I brought each of my children home, love knots often threatened to strangle me. Earaches, colds, sore throats, cuts and bruises, even broken bones tore at my heartstrings of love. Sometimes I became irritable or weepy at the end of a day. These are the day's my love knots had me questioning my ability to be a mom.

As mothers we feel a *right* to fight some our children's battles during their growing up years. I marched to school to defend my children or stood between them and the bully. I waited in the rain with an umbrella at the bus stop. I advocated for them in a doctor's office, felt the sting of necessary baby shots and cheered them on in every endeavor in which they attempted to succeed.

I think most mothers are really devoted and tied with such love for their children that they would give themselves up to danger in a heartbeat to save their child. The love knots squirm in our hearts when we watch our children ride a two-wheel bike for the first time or listen to their giggle when introduced to the sandpaper kisses of a kitty, sloppy one from a puppy. We think nothing of the thump-thump, to which out chest wall gives way, when our children sob over a lost friend or first love. It seems like the squeeze never ends as our children's lives go along without bumps. Then the knots tighten again when we feel we can't bear to see them hurt or disappointed.

When my kids went off to college I wanted to go with them. Instead, I tucked money between the clothes in their suitcases. I packed stationary with a note asking them to write, to please call me every day and when I closed and zipped their bags, I collapsed in the privacy of my room and wept for hours.

I sat by the phone. I rushed to the mailbox. Worry laced my love knots. *I hope they set alarms so they get up in time for classes. There is so much danger in our world. Will they be careful? Will they be able to drive in the traffic of the big city? Who will do their laundry? Are they going to eat right? What if they get into the wrong crowd? Who will turn out the lights in their rooms when they fall asleep? What if, what if?*

My children, all grown up now, never leave my thoughts. I probably missed some significant moments in my children's lives. I've wrestled with love knot feelings that I may have failed them in some way. I'm sure I fell short in the parenting scene at times, but I hope the love I showed my children has made my shortcomings easy for them to forget.

I take note of my cesarean scar and the shiny stretch marks and I think of them as badges of honor. Where are the medals of heroism and courage for mothers? Firemen, policemen, and soldiers often wear badges of honor. I haven't seen crowds of people applauding or shaking the hands of mothers, giving mothers recognition publically. Mother's more or less slip through life as mothers. Mother's carry love knots secretly hidden in their hearts. Mother's are the unsung heroes.

My children are on their own love journey. My oldest daughter has three children and she has often shared that until she became a mother she never understood the joys, fears and disappointments of motherhood. I have a feeling that her heart has knotted more than a few times as a mother.

My son won't feel the love knots of a mother. I am certain however that all the love he experiences in his lifetime will change his heart in so many ways. He will become stronger in his appreciation of family, which is already important for him.

I don't know if my youngest daughter will become a mother, but her love experiences will produce a stronger, more secure young woman.

Besides my faith, my children are the anchors of my life. I try not to worry about what they may become, but remember who they are today. I am thankful the love knots a mother harbors will never go away.

Alice Klies

54

Little Nudgings

I took a trip out of town for a week of training. Being with like-minded individuals who understood the pressures of my day job as an Activities Director in a Nursing Home was wonderful. Following a particularly long and intensive day of classes, I needed a change in my routine. After discussing Death and Dying for our last class, I did not want to return to my hotel room and stare at the four walls.

Many times I have fought with the despair of depression, thinking of what I learned in class about those subjects. But on this particular day I was in a contented mindset.

Driving down a few exits, I came to a row of chain restaurants and chose one that was not too busy on that Veteran's Day. I enjoyed a wonderful meal and the company of the novel I'd taken with me.

I signed the receipt for my bill and turned the page to finish the chapter I was reading. Looking up, I was taken aback to discover a woman sitting across from me. Where had she come from?

"I know this is weird," she said, "but, God laid it on my heart to come over here."

I could see that she was nervous, not knowing what my reaction might be. Well, I felt somewhat better. At least she was a believer.

"I've never done anything like this before, but God kept pressuring me and…well, I had to obey."

I wanted to applaud her and put her at ease. I had no idea what she was about to say, but I planned to listen.

"I just want you to know that you are absolutely beautiful. God loves you — and I don't know what you're going through — but he has not forgotten you."

Tears welled in my eyes. God knew I needed this message, even when I didn't. "Thank you. I appreciate it." I smiled, longing to put her uneasiness at rest.

"God Bless."

We both bestowed the blessing, before she returned to a nearby table. I noticed as she returned to her seat that a man, probably her husband, had been anxiously watching our interaction.

Closing my eyes, I thanked God for the reminder of his love. There have been many years when I've felt as if I were in a waiting pattern. I was thankful for the reminder that not only did God love me, but he had not forgotten me.

Waving goodbye to the young couple, I prayed that God would bless them for their faithfulness to his nudging.

How many times do we listen to the little nudgings from God in our life, nudgings that might become a blessing to others?

Diana Leagh Matthews

55

Butterflies from Heaven

Death is never easy, but when you lose a child death takes hold and never leaves. I recently lost my youngest daughter to death. She was twenty-seven with her whole life ahead of her, but death took her from the loving security of my arms and from her family.

Michelle became sick when she was eighteen, and for almost ten years she refused to take her medication so she deteriorated. I didn't approve of her lifestyle and pushed her out of my life.

The phone call came five weeks before she died. "Momma, I want to come home. I'm dying."

My heart wrenched, my stomach knotted and my throat closed. Tears fell like rain against my face. I blamed myself for not believing her. She had a proclivity for lying and now it was probably too late to take back all the years of hurt and distrust.

I hung up the phone and turned to my husband. I didn't have to say anything. He took me in his arms and we cried together. "My baby is dying," was all I could say.

When we arrived at the bus station Michelle was unrecognizable. She was a skeleton of the beautiful woman I had seen five months before.

She had come home to die. I was angry with myself, with her, and with God. How could He let this happen?

She barely had the strength to stand. My mind was a whirlwind of emotions. Anger and sadness peppered my thoughts. I shook off my negative thoughts and reached out. Her twig-thin arms wrapped around my neck and the tears flowed down my face. "Don't cry momma. I'm home. I'm home," her rasped voice whispered against my tear-soaked face. She had come home to die.

We sat in silence on the long drive home. I didn't know what to say as anger boiled up inside of me. This would be our last drive home together and I couldn't even say one word.

Within a week she was rushed to the hospital. Fear overtook me. I didn't want to hear what I knew in my heart. I couldn't cope and refused to make any premature decisions. I had to believe she would get well.

My family and I gathered in the stark waiting area and talked about the good times. We talked about how much my daughter loved to sing and how she loved life. I wanted to forget her frail shell of a body was lying in a hospital bed hooked up to machines.

The dreaded time finally came. The doctor came and told us, "Michelle's body is shutting down." His words echoed in a distant fog. What was he saying? Words like metastasized, full-blown AIDS, and hospice were flowing from his lips.

My knees gave out and I crumbled into a chair. He was sending her home to die. I refused to accept what the doctor said. I began to pray for a miracle, although I didn't expect a miracle would come.

While Michelle was in the hospital, her dad painted her bedroom pink and decorated the walls with butterflies. He didn't want her to come home to stark white walls. She always wanted to be free like a butterfly, but now her wings were clipped and she could no longer soar high in the sky.

Her eyes lit up the moment she saw her room. For an instant, I thought I could see a glimmer of hope. Maybe she wouldn't give up on her life.

But maybes aren't enough, and my beautiful butterfly had no will to live.

It was hard to settle into the countdown weeks. Every day, I grew angrier. I was angry with God, but angrier with myself for all the years I had lost withou her. I could never make up for the wedge forged between us. I didn't know how much time we would have, but I had to make it special for my daughter. While she still had her faculties, we colored, we talked, and we remembered the good times.

One morning, needing a break from the waiting game, I went onto my back deck and sat in the early-morning silence. No birds chirped, just quietness. I closed my eyes, lifted my face toward Heaven and prayed. "Lord, I know my baby is going to die. Please keep her safe in your loving arms."

I felt something on my hand. My eyes flew open to find a beautiful butterfly flitting its wings on my hand. The Lord had answered my prayer. Maybe I could find the strength to get through her last days.

The days became long, the nights sleepless, waiting and watching. I prayed she could give me one last Mother's Day together. She did and we made the best of those precious last memories. Her laughter filled the emptiness of my heart.

Week one came and went, but it seemed like an eternity. She became quite and withdrawn. Her body rejected her pain medication. Three more weeks and a skeleton replaced what used to be my daughter. She drifted in and out of a medical induced coma. I sat by her side day and night, no sleep, stroking her face and rubbing her brittle thin hair. "I love you, beautiful butterfly," I whispered against her ear. No longer did she respond, but I knew she heard the words of love.

The hospice nurse warned me. "Anytime, Mrs. Elliott." A feeling of dread swept through my soul when I woke up that day. The nurse came and didn't have to say anything. The pain was written on her face. The inevitable would happen any time. My family gathered by Michelle's side. She gasped her last word, "Momma."

I placed my arms around her. "I love you too Michelle." Then my precious child took her last breath.

The five days that followed her death were a blur. Arrangements had to be made, things had to get done, but I wanted to crawl under the covers and sleep away what was happening. I didn't want to be strong.

I don't know how I made it through her memorial service. My other children, my husband, and grandson surrounded me as we said our final good-byes. When it was over, I wanted to be alone and slipped out onto the back deck. I screamed at God. "Why did you let this happen to my baby?"

I didn't expect Him to answer. But suddenly several butterflies danced passed me, flitting back and forth. A beautiful black and yellow one landed on my tear-streaked face. At that moment, I knew God hadn't taken my daughter to hurt me; he took her so she would never suffer again.

Now, whenever my grandson sees a butterfly, he runs to me and asks, "Mawma, is that Aunt Michelle?"

I smile. "Yes Cameron, that beautiful butterfly from heaven is a gift from Aunt Michelle.

Debra Elliott

56

Expressions of Love

We had practiced the songs faithfully, excited to express our love and devotion to our Heavenly Father through music as part of the Christmas program. Our director gave us last-minute instructions in the practice room: When the audience was seated, the choir would quietly walk down the church's center aisle.

Anticipation swelled in the sanctuary.

As we started down the aisle, a small voice called for all to hear, "Hi, Grandmother!"

Lacy, my three-year-old granddaughter, was excited to let me know she was there. Happy to see me, her three-year-old mind didn't comprehend that this was a solemn occasion.

Her mother quickly quieted her amid smiles and muffled giggles erupting in the audience and choir.

Lacy's face beamed when I smiled at her from the platform. I was surprised and thrilled she recognized me.

During the entire evening, my heart remained warm with Lacy's expression of love. After the program, many people commented on her greeting.

"How sweet that your granddaughter recognized you."

"Her face was shining when she hollered at you."

"You're certainly special to her."

"It's wonderful how our grandchildren express their love for us."

A child responds unabashedly to love and attention from a parent, grandparent, teacher, friend, or neighbor. Hugs, smiles, and waves are given freely to the recipient. They delight in coloring pictures and making items to give to someone who loves them. They are not ashamed of showing their devotion. Openness is their mode of operation.

As a child of God, I am loved even more dearly than I can possibly love Lacy. God sent his Son to die for me. He chose me, has a plan for my life, and made me with my unique talents and personality. He is my Protector, Guide, Teacher, Wisdom, and Savior.

At various times, I have been guilty of not openly expressing my love and devotion to my loving God. I have allowed concern about my reputation and popularity to keep me from expressing my love to Him. Because of perceived persecution from others, I haven't spoken up for him. Fear of losing prestige has overruled my desire to share about God's help and guidance.

Jesus enjoyed little children coming to Him. Jesus said in Matthew 19:14 (NLT), "Let the children come to me. Don't stop them! For the kingdom of Heaven belongs to such as these."

I am reminded to express my devotion for and to him in the same way as a small child — exuberantly, freely, frequently and fearlessly — as easily as Lacy expressed her love for me.

Helen L. Hoover

57
A Love So True

There's something about the outside of a horse
that's good for the inside of a person.
Winston Churchill

Regalo, meaning *gift* in Spanish, was a present from my parents. It was love at first sight...after visiting many Peruvian Paso horse ranches on the mainland.

In Regalo, I found a soul mate. Woman and beast, friends and companions. For sixteen years, my stallion and I glided over any accessible path, trail, or dirt road on all corners of the Big Island of Hawaii and Kauai. I loved to jump on Regalo bareback with only a halter, and when heading home, gallop full speed up the hill. The warm sweat of his horsepower glued me to his back and left a stain on my clothes that rarely washed away.

After a day apart, my heart would sing upon returning home to him. Wrapping my arms around his massive neck and hugging him closely was a prerequisite to rubbing my face up and down his soft nose. "Hijo, (red) I love your hejo (nose)," I crooned.

Each morning, my heart fluttered at the sound of his soft nicker, as he watched me approach carrying his feed bucket. Though some horses chew voraciously in their zest, Regalo savored each bite, which he masticated to a pulp. The sound of his giant molars penetrating a compressed cube of alfalfa played a symphony to my ears.

Regalo's cashmere-like lips caressed my palm, as he gently plucked a banana or carrot from my hand. I gathered fruits to tantalize his taste buds including stalks of bananas I chopped to the ground with a machete. A pail full of ripe mangoes or papayas slurped and sucked to the last drop, a five-gallon bucket of water gulped to the bottom on a hot day, further serenaded me. The eventual discarded waste product of digested hay or sweet feed intoxicated my nostrils.

Gentle nipping while tickling me with fine tipped whiskers was an expression of affection such as is common between horses. Perched on a bucket under Regalo's neck or next to his eleven-hundred-pound mass of muscle, I felt no fear. Many a tranquil sunset we enjoyed together while I scratched his itchy spots with a long wooden drink stirrer I kept in a guava tree.

I was more than happy to soothe him. He raised his head and scrunched his lips in agreement, after his nose guided me where to scratch next. If I paused too long, a slight nudge kept me in motion.

Trust remained true between us. The memory and spirit of his presence will remain with me forever.

Andrea Cronrod

58

A Guarded Heart

When my husband and I lived in France, there was an ancient city I wanted to visit. A city we'd driven past on several occasions. But, we were always on our way to or from a basketball game, and, much to my regret, we never found the time to stop.

Last summer I finally got to check that visit off my bucket list.

Carcassonne is an old fortified city that stands like a beacon on a hilltop. A fairy-tale, Cinderella city with turrets and barbicans and stone laid streets that, if you closed your eyes and imagined it, you would feel quite certain that a horse-mounted knight-in-shining-armor would clip clop past you at any moment.

As romantic as it is to imagine life in those days, God had a few thoughts of his own to speak into my soul that day. Starting with a whispered "Guard your heart..."

I have loved those words from Proverbs since I first heard them many years ago. But, being reminded of them again in such an imposing city like ancient Carcassonne, made the words spring to life for me.

The city is well over two thousand years old. In fact, most scholars believe it to have been established around the year 100 B.C. History tells of a King Pepin the Short, who had conquered most of France during his reign. But he could not penetrate the impregnable fortress of Carcassonne. To this day, it is still protected by its two outer walls and fifty-three watchtowers.

Walking between those two massive walls, I couldn't help but think about a man in the Bible who knew a thing or two about building walls like these. Nehemiah. He wrote this about his experience:

So we rebuilt the wall until all of it reached half its height, for the people worked with all their heart. Our enemies plotted together to come and fight and stir up trouble. But we prayed to our God and posted a guard day and night to meet this threat. I devoted myself to the work on the wall. The enemy continued his schemes. They tried to frighten us, but I prayed, "Strengthen my hands."

So the wall was completed. Our enemies were defeated, realizing that it had been done with the help of our God.

Nehemiah 4:6-15 [Author's paraphrase]

As I swept my fingertips along one of those thick stone walls, I wondered, *How well am I guarding my heart from outer influences that seek to stir up trouble in my life? What sneaks in when my guard is down? Skepticism? Cynicism? Doubt? Fear? Lord, please help me post a guard day and night to meet this threat.*

Thoughts of guards caused my eyes to turn upward toward the tall, commanding watchtowers where many of them would have been stationed. That would be quite a climb, but Rey and I decided to wind our way up to the top of one of them.

When we reached the top we could see for miles. We had a bird's-eye view. Nothing could have escaped the eyes of a watchman up in this post, unless he wasn't paying attention or paid no heed at all.

As I thought about that, I was reminded of a dialogue between Ezekiel and God, that went something like this:

Ezekiel: "What if the guard sees the enemy coming, but doesn't blow the trumpet?"

God: "Since that guard didn't warn the people...he will be held responsible for whatever disaster befalls them. You, son of man, are the watchman!"

Ezekiel 33:6-7 [Author's paraphrase]

You...are the watchman!

I put my hand to my heart as I stood looking over the wide landscape. What a visual God had given me. I am the watchman of my heart. God will hold me responsible for what I let into it and what I don't. If I choose to ignore or disregard those things that lay siege against it, if I fail to keep it undefiled by sin or undisturbed by trouble, I can also expect, as the watchman in Ezekiel's day did, painful consequences to follow.

That's because our hearts are dear to God. That's the reason it's so important that we keep our hearts safe just as we would a precious jewel.

The reason we guard our hearts is because from it flows the issues of life. The issues of life — our actions, works, pursuits, and dreams — all proceed from the heart. When a heart is well kept it will not only flow fresh with life-giving healing and wholeness to us, but it will also bring solace to others, and more importantly, bring glory to the God who made us.

As Rey and I wandered into the center of Carcassonne we discovered a large church. Its towers, too, reach skyward. It dawned on me as I stood under its lofty ceiling, that the folks who built this city understood, as Nehemiah had understood, that beyond their own strength and resolve, beyond any wall or tower they could build, God was their most important ally.

Placing God in the heart of the city was a constant reminder to them that they had an infinitely more valuable resource at their disposal. They had prayer. They had a precious friend and Savior they could turn to when they were under attack. A heavenly Father who would hear them when they called for his aid and move on their behalf.

Keeping our hearts diligently in touch with God through prayer is vital to thwarting the enemy's schemes. And with his help, any outside influences that seek our undoing will be defeated and, as in Nehemiah's life, others will see how precious God is.

The sun was setting as Rey and I walked through the last archway out of Carcassonne. God had one final love gift waiting for me.

Passing out through the gateway stood a stone Cross. I stopped to take a picture. Then I bowed my head in prayer. How blessed I felt that God has whispered love to my heart that day.

Above all else, guard your heart, for from it flows the issues of life.
Proverbs 4:23 [Author's paraphrase]

Julie Miller

59

A Click Away

After checking my inbox for emails I check the junk box for spam. Most are emails I don't want so I simply click and delete forever. Ah! No spam.

But whenever I look to see if there are more, I'm not surprised to see that there are. Some are from the same sender; some look like another person has been hacked. Many are undesirable. Most are ridiculous offers, and some think I'm lonely or looking for the greatest item ever.

No matter how often, or how much I delete forever, others keep coming in. It's kind of like my life. I've learned a lot in the many decades I've been living. I have grown wiser, know more about myself and the Lord.

And yet, no matter how much I learn, in my personal life there always seems to be more spam or junk. I ask forgiveness for unforgiveness, procrastination, or sins of commission and omission. I get the forgiveness, but before long my life has more junk.

Sometimes it stays much too long before I delete. Some just seem to keep returning.

Wouldn't it be nice if we could click our personal boxes, and the boxes of other sinners out there, and the spam be deleted forever?

Oh! Wait a minute. Didn't Jesus delete those sins once and for all when he died on the cross?

Yes, he did. Our sins are forgiven. But he says, "Be perfect." That means, although we're forgiven, we need to keep deleting forever all that junk in our spam box when it pops up. There will always be more. But there is always the sacrifice Jesus made that covers the more.

He promised to give us abundant life. And yet, we face difficulties. Read what Anonymous wrote about things we experience. It's as if Jesus is talking to us.

If you never felt pain
Then how would you know
That I am a healer?

If you have never prayed through
How would you know
That I am a deliverer?

If you never had a trial
How could you call yourself
An overcomer?

If you never felt sadness
How would you know
That I am a comforter?

If you never made a mistake
How would you know
That I am forgiving?

If you knew it all
How would you know
That I will answer your questions?

If you never were in trouble
How would you know
That I will come to your rescue?

If you were never broken
Then how would you know
That I can make you whole?

If you never had a problem
How would you know
That I can solve them?

If you never had any suffering
Then how would you know
What I went through?

If you never went through the fire
Then how would you
Become pure?

If I gave you all things
How would you
Appreciate them?

If you had all power
Then how would you learn
To depend on me?

If your life was perfect
Then what would you
Need me for?

If I never corrected you
How would you know
That I love you?

Q. How do we know Jesus loves us?

A. The Bible tells us so.

Q. How can we show our love for him?

A. The Book of Love tells us, in the chapter on love —
1 Corinthians 13

Q. What is love?

A. Love is action.

Q. What is love in action?

A. Jesus admonishes us to love ourselves, and love others that
same way.

So, let's just keep deleting the junk and spam in our lives, and concentrate
on the good things the Lord puts into our heart's inbox.

And enjoy those Loving Moments.

Yvonne Lehman

About the Authors

Ellen Andersen grew up in California and has lived in Greenville, South Carolina since 2002. She loves to garden. Ellen serves in her church as a Stephen Minister. She can relate to and minister to others who are hurting since she deals with ongoing physical issues of her own. Ellen has published several devotions online at christiandevotions.us. Connect with her at www. ellenandersen.blogspot.com or on Twitter at @EllenAndersenSC.

Sheryl M. Baker is a wife, mother, and grandmother. She lives in northwest Indiana with her husband, Ben. During the day she works as a customer service specialist. With her writing, she enjoys bringing hope and encourage through God's word. Her devotions have been published in *Power for Today, Light from the Word* and *Christiandevotions.us*. Her story, "Mollie's Tale," is included in *Spoken Moments* and "Make Peace with the Past" is in *More Christmas Moments*. She maintains a weekly blog, *Spun by the Potter: Discovering God in Everyday Life*. To see more of Sheryl's writing, visit spunbythepotter.com.

Robin Bayne is an award-winning author of 17 novels, novellas and short stories. She compiled a collection of devotions for writers titled *Words to Write By*. She lives in Maryland with her husband of 25 years. Visit her at www. robinbayne.com.

Mason K Brown's writings have been published in six volumes of *Chicken Soup for the Soul, Guideposts, When God Makes Lemonade, RAIN Magazine 2013* and *2014, Vista* (12 times), *The Secret Place* (8 times), *The Mother's Heart Magazine, Help! I'm a Parent, God Makes Lemonade, CAP Connection, Apple Hill Cider Press, Seeds of... a Collection of Writings by Pacific Northwest Authors* and others. She writes the monthly columns "Zap, Kackle, Plop" and "Out of the Ark" for *The Lincoln City News Guard*. The release of *Jesus Encounters* (2015) includes her latest published work.

Elsie H. Brunk and her husband of 57 years have four children, 12 grandchildren and four great-grandchildren. Her devotions and articles have been published in *Christian Parenting Today, Live, The Family Digest, Standard, The Secret Place* and other periodicals. Her book, *Streams of Living Water for a Thirsty Soul,* is available as an ebook. Elsie's stories, "Grandchild Journal — Legacy of Love" and "The Roses" are included in *Precious, Precocious Moments.* "A Fresh New Christmas" is in *More Christmas Moments.* Visit Elsie on her website: elsiebrunk.com.

LeAnn Campbell is married to Bud. They have six adult children and numerous grandchildren and great grandchildren. LeAnn resumed her college education at age 40 and is a retired special education teacher. Her published works include over 1600 articles and stories, two devotional books published by Extreme Diva Media, and a series of mysteries for middle-grade readers. Four of the books (*Century Farm* series) have been published by OakTara, with two more awaiting publication. Her blog on Preserving Family Memories is at www.leanncampbell.com.

Rebecca Carpenter writes at her lake retreat near Orlando. After retiring from teaching elementary school, she and her husband traveled the world for missions and pleasure. Experiences with her granddaughters, traveling, and nature inspire her writings. Her articles have appeared in *Adventures in Odyssey Clubhouse* magazine, *Posh Parenting, Christmas Moments, Celebrating Christmas with...Memories, Poetry, and Good Food,* and several local publications. After losing her husband and both parents within months, she wrote page after page of her grief journey. Forty of those devotionals will be released in a book this year. You may visit her at http://rebeccacarpenter.blogspot.com.

John Chaney is a first-time author of "God, the Cosmos, and Me." He hails from Louisville, Kentucky. His earlier aspirations were to be a professional musician (drums) but decided on a business degree from Transylvania University in Lexington, Kentucky. He worked in many fields, such as insurance, automotive, restaurant, customer service and temporary work. Although he has never worked directly in the ministry, he is an "on-fire" Christian for God and Jesus Christ, and stands "always ready to minister or otherwise talk Bible!" Recently, he is a desktop student of skygazing/astronomy/physics, aviation/air traffic control, playing the banjo, programming music, writing, walking, and bicycling. He attends Bible studies and studies the Bible on his own in his adopted town of Carmel, Indiana with his wife Angie and three cats.

Josh Clevenger is the pastor of Cory Zion Church in Cory, Indiana. He is a husband, father, pastor, author, and evangelist. Josh has numerous books in publication, along with an active outreach ministry. He wants people to feel connected to God's grace and experience the comfort of His mercies. Follow Josh Clevenger Ministries to get daily encouragement from the Lord.

Andrea Cronrod - After many years passionately and vigorously breeding and raising horses, physical burnout changed Andrea's focus from active to sedentary, creatures to divine. Her etheric stallion comrade, Regalo, stolen by the hand of a devastating accident, taught Andrea how to love. The worship of a horse, developed into relationship with God, never to leave or forsake her.

Jeanne Doyon encourages us to draw nearer to the Lover of our soul through her ministry, *Pausing to See God Clearly*. She *connects the truths in Scripture to the ordinary events of life and shares her reflections in* her blog. She teaches at women's retreats and events. Jeanne enjoys photography, tea, time with friends, journaling, and being with her Heavenly Father. She and her husband John live in Connecticut. They have three grown children and a daughter-in-love, all who live too far away. Contact her at jeanne.doyon@gmail.com and visit www. JeanneDoyon.com to find out more about her ministry. You can also find and follow Jeanne on social media: Facebook: www.facebook.com/jeannedoyon. writer.speaker. LinkedIn: www.linkedin.com/in/jeannedoyon - Twitter: www. Twitter.com/jeannedoyon. Pinterest: www.pinterest.com/inspireshope.

Kristin Tobin Dossett lives in Kentucky with her husband of seven years and their three young boys. She has a Master of Science in Nursing degree from Vanderbilt University and works as a nurse practitioner in a pediatric primary care clinic. She blogs at www.lovemercywalkhumbly.com. She can be reached at kristindossett@gmail.com.

Terri Elders received her first byline, published in 1946 on the children's page of the *Portland Oregonian,* on a piece about how bats saved her family's home from fire. At nine years old, she hadn't known that her title, "Bats in Our Belfry," would lead readers to suspect her family's sanity. Her stories have appeared in over 100 anthologies. She can be contacted at telders@hotmail.com.

Debra Elliott is a published author living in Alabama with her husband of 30 years. She has three grown children and two grandchildren. Her works appear in several Christian anthologies.

Georgia Florey-Evans is new to the Christian romantic suspense genre, having previously written and published two series of contemporary romances. In her new series, *In Shadow*, she feels called to share her beliefs in the midst of drawing readers into the story. The best compliment she gets is, "That could happen to me." She is a member of ACFW, and has one short story "Gotcha!" which was short-listed on the international Writer's Village contest two years ago. While not writing, she enjoys spending time with her retired husband, walking her puppy, Gizmo, and reading. They make their home in the small town they were raised in, and are thankful all six of their grandchildren live nearby. John Lucious Evans would be thirty years old now, but she believes she'll hold him one day. Sharing her story was difficult and painful, but she hopes it shows others how strong God's love is. She can be reached on her website, www.georgiaevansauthor.com.

Dorothy Floyd has made her home in Augusta, Georgia for over 20 years. Life as a single mom and a special education teacher is both challenging and rewarding. In the next few years, Dorothy plans to retire from teaching and publish her collection of devotional stories taken from life experiences.

Janice S. Garey lives in Atlanta with husband Art, and Miss Bosley, a stray kitten who arrived for Christmas 2013 in a divine moment. Janice's publishing credits include book reviews, an article in *Church Libraries*, and an article in the *Christian Library International* (CLI) newsletter about the need for Spanish language Bibles in prisons. As a CLI volunteer she hopes to reach prisoners and the world with God's word. She loves co-teaching first through sixth grade Sunday school and treasures Women's Missionary Union relationships. She takes writing courses with Christian Writers Guild.

Theresa Jenner Garrido was born and raised in the beautiful Pacific Northwest. She graduated from the University of Washington with a degree in English, taught middle school language arts, social studies, and drama for over 25 years then retired early to devote time and energy to her passion of writing. She has traveled extensively throughout the United States, Canada and abroad. She currently resides in South Carolina with her retired engineer husband, a rescue dog named Molly and a stray black cat, who morphs into a panther whenever provoked.

Dianna Good is a retired English teacher of 25 years. She has been journaling and writing for years, mostly for her own enjoyment of reliving and discovering life. She was encouraged to join Northern Arizona's Word Weavers and has appreciated the talent of those around her. Dianna has been blessed with her husband and best friend of 36 years, two grown children, and four beautiful grandchildren.

Carol Graham is the author of an award-winning memoir, *Battered Hope*, the blog *Never Ever Give Up Hope*, and a regular contributor to numerous blog sites. She has a monthly column in *Book Fun Magazine* and is published in several anthologies including a bestseller. In 2015, Carol received the *Woman of Impact Award* from *Focus on Women Magazine* and Author of the Year for her memoir, *Battered Hope*. Carol hosts the bi-weekly talk show *Never Ever Give*

Up Hope, interviewing people with remarkable stories of how they conquered overwhelming obstacles and achieved success. *Never Ever Give Up Hope* has an international audience in over 70 countries. In addition to motivational speaking, hosting a talk show and writing, Carol is a business owner, a wife, mother, grandmother, and together with her husband has rescued over 30 dogs.

Kay Harper spent her childhood exploring, 20s rebelling, 30s on a quest, 40s in Never-Never Land and 50s lost and found. Through it all her pen has been a trusted companion. Kay has published several of her award-winning short stories online and the old fashioned way. She writes from her home in Florida, minutes from the white-sand beaches of the Gulf of Mexico.

Lydia E. Harris has been married to her college sweetheart, Milt, for 47 years. They have two married children and five grandchildren ranging from preschool to high school. Lydia earned a Master of Arts degree in home economics. She has written numerous articles, book reviews, devotionals, and stories. Focus on the Family's *Clubhouse* magazines for children publish her recipes, which she develops and tests with her grandchildren. She writes the column, "A Cup of Tea with Lydia," and is called Grandma Tea by her grandchildren. Lydia has contributed to numerous books and is author of *Preparing My Heart for Grandparenting: For Grandparents at Any Stage of the Journey.*

Lori Hatcher is a blogger, inspirational speaker, and author of the Christian Small Publisher's 2016 Book of the Year, *Hungry for God...Starving for Time, Five-Minute Devotions for Busy Women.* A Toastmasters International contest-winning speaker, Lori's goal is to help busy women connect with God in the craziness of everyday life. She especially loves small children, furry animals, and chocolate. You'll find her pondering the marvelous and the mundane on her blog, *Hungry for God...Starving for Time.*

Judith Victoria Hensley is a multi-award-winning retired middle school teacher, weekly newspaper columnist for the *Harland Daily Enterprise,* freelance writer, photographer, speaker, and Christian blogger of *Queen of Ordinary and One Step Beyond the Door.* She has authored and edited a dozen books on Appalachian folklore and published two middle school chapter books. Her magazine articles and short stories have appeared in a variety of publications. From her home in the Kentucky highlands, she is writing Inspirational Romance novels.

Helen L. Hoover enjoys sewing, reading, knitting, and traveling. She and her husband are retired, live in Northwest Arkansas and volunteer at a Christian college. They are blessed with two grown children, four grandchildren and four great-grandchildren. Helen's devotions and personal stories are published in books and Christian handout papers.

Cynthia Howerter, an award-winning writer, utilizes her education and training from Penn State University, Villanova University, and Christian Communicators in everything she tackles. Descended from a Revolutionary War hero and a member of the Daughters of the American Revolution (DAR), she loves writing about the colonial period. Her unpublished historical novel won First Place at the 2015 Florida Christian Writers Conference, and her non-fiction anthology book, *God's Provision in Tough Times*, co-authored with La-Tan Roland Murphy, was a 2014 Selah award finalist. A versatile speaker, she enjoys enthralling audiences with a variety of topics that include faith-inspiring life experiences and our exciting American history. Cynthia and her husband live in Virginia.

Amanda Hughes holds a Master of Arts in Christian Education from Southwestern Baptist Theological Seminary. She serves as Outreach Director for Constituting America, and enjoys encouraging others through her writing on faith and freedom at her blog www.AmandaHughesWriter.com. She lives in Washington, D.C., and is writing her first book.

Alice Klies is a freelance writer, member of Northern Arizona's Word Weavers International and has been published in *WordSmith Journal*. Her stories, "Just Us Girls" and "The Dog Did What?" are published in *Chicken Soup for the Soul*. Other stories appearing in anthologies include "Grandfather, Father and Me," "Grandmother, Mother and Me," "God Still Meets Needs," and "Friends of Faith." Guideposts published "Angels on Earth." Alice is writing a memoir.

Nancy Julien Kopp is originally from Chicago but has lived in the Flint Hills of Kansas for many years. She writes creative nonfiction, memoir, inspirational, award winning children's fiction, poetry and articles on the writing craft. She's published in eighteen *Chicken Soup for the Soul* books, other anthologies, newspapers, ezines and internet radio. She blogs about her writing world with tips and encouragement for writers at www.writergrannysworld.blogspot.com.

Barbara Latta is a free-lance writer whose passion is to share how the grace of God can free us from the rules of religious tradition. Her articles, devotions, and poems have been published in newspapers, magazines, and websites. She writes a monthly column for the *Pike Journal-Reporter* in Zebulon, Georgia.

She is a board member of the East Metro Atlanta Christian Writers. She enjoys riding motorcycles with her Harley husband, and their biker travels are the inspiration for her blog, *Navigating Life's Curves*, at barbaralatta. blogspot.com.

Marcia Lee Laycock lives in central Alberta, Canada with her pastor/husband and two incorrigible golden retrievers. She has lived in Canada's Arctic (Dawson City, Yukon), and two degrees off the equator (Papua, New Guinea), which have given her much fodder for her writing and speaking ministry. Her work has won several awards, been endorsed by Janette Oke, Phil Callaway, Mark Buchanan and Sigmund Brouwer, and has been broadcast on national radio. Visit Marcia's website at www.marcialeelaycock.com.

Yvonne Lehman is author of 57 novels. She founded, and directed for 25 years, the Blue Ridge Mountains Christian Writers Conference and now directs the Blue Ridge Novelist Retreat held annually in October at Ridgecrest North Carolina conference center. Her latest books, in addition to the Moments series, are a novella, *Have Dress Will Marry* in the collection, *Heart of a Cowboy*, *Writing Right to Success* (by 25 authors about their journey to success and craft articles) and a cozy mystery, *Better Latte than Never*. Her popular, 50th book is *Hearts that Survive — A Novel of the Titanic*, which signs periodically at the Titanic Museum in Pigeon Forge, Tennessee. Visit her website at: www.yvonnelehman.com

Diana Leagh Matthews is a vocalist, writer, speaker and life coach. She is a graduate of the Christian Communicators Conference and Christian Devotions Boot Camp. She lives in South Carolina and enjoys sharing God's love with others. To learn more about her ministry, check out her websites at www.dianaleaghmatthews and www.alookthrutime.com.

Beverly Hill McKinney has published over three hundred inspirational articles in such publications as *Good Old Days, Breakthrough Intercessor, Just Between Us, Women Alive, P31, and Plus Magazine*. She has devotions in *Cup of Comfort Devotional — Daily Reflections of God's Grace and Love, Open Windows, God Still Meets Needs,* and *God Still Leads and Guides*. Her stories have been featured in anthologies such as *Christmas Miracles, Men of Honor, Guidepost Extraordinary Answers to Prayer, Christian Miracles,* and *Precious, Precocious Moments*. She has also self-published two books, *Through the Parsonage Window* and *Whispers from God, Poems of Inspiration*. She graduated from the Jerry B. Jenkins Christian Writer's Guild and lives in Rogue River, Oregon.

Lenora McWhorter resides in the Chicago area. She is a retired Early Childhood Educator who delights in working with young children. She now spends her time with community activities, church activities, home Bible studies and playing with grandchildren. Her hobbies are writing poetry and coloring. She is a published writer with several Christian publishers of devotionals, poetry, and Sunday school curriculum.

Julie Miller has been inspiring children, youth, and women as a speaker, teacher, quiet day retreat leader, author and mentor for over 30 years. She was the Director of Women's Bible Studies at Eagle Brook Church, is a certified Spiritual Director and the owner of Heart Matters Publishing Company. She is an alumnus of Bethel University and Christos Center for Spiritual Formation. She has written Bible Study curriculum and devotionals, including the collaboration, *Whispers of God's Grace: Stories to Encourage Your Heart.* Julie draws on her wide range of life experiences, humor and love of God's Word and his creation for her writing. When she is not writing, you will find her absorbed in a good book, puttering in her garden or dreaming of France. Julie and her husband, Rey, live in White Bear Lake, Minnesota and are the parents of two grown sons, Erik and Kyle.

Marybeth Mitcham holds a BS in Biology, is completing her MPH in nutrition, and works as tutor for Liberty University's Online Writing Center. She is an emerging freelance author, whose writings have been published online. She was a guest on the Chris Fabry Live radio show, discussing her article, "My Magnum Opus," and is a public speaker for the pro-life movement. Marybeth lives with her family in southern Adirondack region of New York, where she is working on her first book.

Vicki H. Moss is Contributing Editor for *Southern Writers Magazine* and past Editor-at-Large. A columnist for the *American Daily Herald*, she's also a poet, author of *How to Write for Kids' Magazines* and *Writing with Voice*, a Precept Ministries Leader and a Christian Communicators graduate. She has written for *Hopscotch* and *Boy's Quest* magazines for the last decade in addition to being published in *Christmas Moments, Divine Moments* and *Precious, Precocious Moments,* South West Writer's *The Sage, Country Woman, In the City, Borderlines,* Scotland's *Thistle Blower,* and *I Believe in Heaven.* She was selected to be a presenter of her fiction and creative nonfiction short stories for three conferences in a row at the Southern Women Writers Conference held at Rome, Georgia's Berry College. Vicki is also a speaker and on faculty for writers conferences. For more information visit livingwaterfiction.com.

Marilyn Nutter of Greer, South Carolina is the author of three devotional books and a contributor to online sites and compilations. She is a Bible teacher and speaker for women's community and church groups, a grief support facilitator, and serves on the women's ministry council at her church. Visit www.marilynnutter.com or contact marilynnutter@gmail.com.

Colleen L. Reece describes herself as an ordinary person with an extraordinary God. Raised in a home without electricity or running water but filled with love for God and family, Colleen learned to read by kerosene lamplight and dreamed of someday writing a book. God had multiplied her "someday" book into *150 Books You Can Trust*, with six million copies sold.

Phyllis A. Robeson, born and raised in San Jose, California, earned a bachelor of fine arts degree (majoring in art history and watercolor) at the University of Nebraska, in Lincoln, where she presently resides. She married a career U.S. Army officer/aviator (now retired) and has one daughter. Phyllis writes because of the encouragement of family and friends, and in the process she has published a number of articles in national publications. She loves working with color in decorating, painting, the garden, and has also been a member of a floral arrangers guild.

Toni Armstrong Sample retired early to Greenwood, South Carolina at the end of a successful career as a Human Resource Executive, with the final 15 years as the Owner/President of an HR Consulting and Training firm that she founded. Toni has written for professional journals, recreational magazines, devotionals, newspapers, and inspirational story publications. Her first inspirational romance novel, *The Glass Divider*, was released in 2014 followed by *Transparent Web of Dreams*, *Distortion*, and *A Still Small Voice*. Two novels, *The Soup Kitchen Gala* and *The Song of My Soul* are scheduled for release in 2017, along with her first non-fiction book, *I'll Never Be the Same*. Toni is a Christian Retreat leader, conference speaker, Christian Education and Women's Bible Study facilitator. She is a Commission Artist concentrating on the painting of biblical scenes and characters.

Karen Sawyer is a writer whose work has appeared in *Precious, Precocious Moments*, *Wounded Women of the Bible*, *The Secret Place Devotional*, guest posts in *Mother Inferior* blog and *Unsent Letters* blog, *Girlfriend 2 Girlfriend* magazine, and *Montrose Anytime* magazine. She has contributed 19 articles to *ehow*, and numerous articles for Demand Media's other web based sites. She is a graduate of the Institute of Children's Literature, has a degree in elementary education, and taught elementary school for seven years before her children, now grown, were born. She resides in Austin, Texas with her husband.

Beverly Sce, Ph.D., author, inspirational speaker, founder and director of the Jesus Divine Mercy Ministry has been featured in health care publications and enjoys writing stories that inspire. Her works have appeared in magazines and books including, *Reminisce* and *The Extraordinary Presence of God*. She is a member of the Pearl S. Buck Writers Guild and was published in the inaugural edition of the *Pearl S. Buck Literary Journal*. Beverly has completed the Amherst Writers and Artists Training Program and is certified to use the Amherst Writers and Artists method to lead writing workshops "committed to the belief that a writer is someone who writes and that every writer has a unique voice." She has a passion for cooking and baking "from scratch" which she learned from her mom, enjoys travel, and is an avid reader and quilter who loves hand applique and making Broderie Perse quilts. Born and raised in New Jersey, Beverly and her husband Doug now call Bucks County, Pennsylvania home. While she holds a Ph.D in Health Psychology/Behavioral Medicine, she is pursuing her writing goal and completing a MFA in creative non-fiction. You may contact her at beverlysce@comcast.net.

Cindy Sproles is an author and speaker. She is the cofounder of Christian Devotions Ministries and the Executive Editor of www.christiandevotions.us and www.inspireafire.com. Cindy is the acquisitions editor for SonRise Books and Straight Street Books, imprints of Lighthouse Publishing of the Carolinas. She teaches at writers conferences and women's conferences nationwide. Her best-selling, award-winning novel, *Mercy's Rain* is followed by *Liar's Winter* (August 2017). Visit Cindy at www.cindysproles.com

Shari Struyk has been writing for as long as she can remember: diaries, notes to boys, poems, prayers, letters and posts. She has written a children's book that is in the "paperback" stage —papers back in the drawer for awhile. She lives in New Jersey, works in sales and design in the family business and moonlights as a small party planner/caterer. Shari loves her four kids, two grown boys and seven-year-old boy/girl twins, making things pretty, feeding people delicious foods, and her Savior. As a single mom, she tries to find balance and "strength for today; bright hope for tomorrow."

Annmarie B. Tait resides in Conshohocken, Pennsylvania with her husband, Joe Beck. In addition to writing stories about her large Irish Catholic family and the memories they made, she enjoys singing and recording Irish and

American folk songs with her husband. Among her other passions are cooking, sewing and crocheting. Annmarie has over 50 stories published in various anthologies including *Chicken Soup for the Soul* and the *Patchwork Path* series. You may contact her at irishbloom@aol.com.

Donn Taylor led an Infantry rifle platoon in the Korean War, served with Army aviation in Vietnam, and worked with air reconnaissance in Europe and Asia. Afterwards, he earned a PhD in English literature (Renaissance) and for 18 years taught literature at two liberal arts colleges. He was chosen by faculty as "Scholar of the Year" at one and by students as "Professor of the Year" at the other. His poetry is collected in his book *Dust and Diamond: Poems of Earth and Beyond*. In addition to his historical novel, *Lightning on a Quiet Night*, he has published two suspense novels and a light-hearted mystery. More are on the way. He is a frequent speaker at writers' conferences and groups. He lives in the woods near Houston, Texas, where he continues to write fiction and poetry, as well as essays on writing, ethical issues, and U.S. foreign policy.

Myrtle V. Thompson (aka Jenny) is a retired missionary. She and her husband served in Pakistan, Iran and the UAE. She has also been an educator, a Bible teacher, a writer and women's conference speaker. Now, at age 88, she loves gardening in her tiny backyard, has a small ministry visiting the elderly in retirement and rehab facilities, and teaches a Sunday School class of "older folks" (doesn't seem to realize she is in that class, too!) She and her husband, who passed away in 2013, are proud parents of 5 children, 17 grandchildren and 6 great grandchildren.

Ann Greenleaf Wirtz is the author of both *Hand of Mercy* and the Bible study that accompanies her new release. She is a public speaker and group study leader. Ann won the Willie Parker Peace History Book Award from the NC Society of Historians for her book *The Henderson County Curb Market*. Her first book, *Sorrow Answered*, was published in 2006. She was published in *More Christmas Moments*, *Chicken Soup for the Soul Christmas*, and locally in the *Times-News*, where she has written over 100 articles. She writes a nostalgic remembrance for *The Pulse* each December, featuring her childhood in Webster Groves, Missouri. Ann is the mother of one very dear son and daughter-in-law, and the grandmother of two delightful grandchildren, a girl and a boy. She is married to her beloved Patrick, and they reside in Hendersonville, North Carolina.

CPSIA information can be obtained
at www.ICGtesting.com
Printed in the USA
FFOW02n0906190917
40108FF

9 781604 950298